Findi. and *Ariminta*

LOVE, LOSS AND SETTLING THE AMERICAN WEST

Byron Burmester

HERITAGE BOOKS
2020

HERITAGE BOOKS

AN IMPRINT OF HERITAGE BOOKS, INC.

Books, CDs, and more—Worldwide

For our listing of thousands of titles see our website
at
www.HeritageBooks.com

Published 2020 by
HERITAGE BOOKS, INC.
Publishing Division
5810 Ruatan Street
Berwyn Heights, Md. 20740

Cover photo: Theodore and Ariminta Burmester
from the collection of the Author.

International Standard Book Number
Paperbound: 978-0-7884-5950-4

To my Mother and Father

Table of Contents

Acknowledgements

There are many people that helped me along the way in the research and writing of this book. Some I have mentioned in the book itself for their assistance or inspiration. However, there are several who I would like to specially thank. First, my Aunt, Anne Bergera, for the initial inspiration. Moreover, since the passing of my mother she has filled that familial void, offering advice and encouragement.

While researching this book I visited a state historical society archive for the first time. I quickly discovered what a valuable resource they are to the researcher. The first one I explored was the Idaho State Historical Society. The men and women there did not just retrieve dusty old documents, they helped me, just a lay researcher, come up with investigating strategies. I would like to thank Peg Shroll and Alisha Graefe for helping me identify photographs and drawings to help flesh out the story. Similarly, I was helped along the way by the Utah State Historical Society and specifically, by Greg Walz. The librarians and archivists at the Taylor Library at the Iliff School of Theology were so thoughtful and helpful. I appreciate the assistance of Erin Shafer and the other archivists there. My friend and colleague, Katie Filler, sacrificed her own personal time to help me edit and offer advice. Finally, I could not do anything without the love and support from my wife, Karen.

fb

Introduction

I loved my father. And like most sons I idealize his best characteristics. My own bias aside, I think most people who knew him would agree that he was a very smart man, and a brilliant storyteller. Perhaps that is where my love for stories comes from. In any event, by the time I returned home from a number of years in the army he was already exhibiting symptoms that would later be diagnosed as amyotrophic lateral sclerosis (A.L.S.) or Lou Gherig's Disease. After the diagnosis, his doctors informed us that he had a rather rare form of the disease that attacked his central nervous system in addition to the usual attack on the extremities. Thus, by the time my father could no longer play his ukulele or properly manipulate dining utensils, his wonderfully sharp intellect and keen wit had shriveled, mimicking that of a seventh grader. At the same time my grandmother, his mother, was also losing her intellectual function and memory simply as a consequence of old age.

Their obvious decline foretold their impending deaths. I dreaded their loss and I knew that with their passing the great stories and personal histories they possessed would be lost forever. So, I began to record the few details they could still access and then I started exploring, searching for extrinsic evidence of their recollections.

Later, when I shared with my aunt and uncle the family history I had uncovered, my aunt told me a family story I had never heard before. My aunt said that my great-great-grandmother, Ariminta Burmester, had been raped and murdered by a ranch hand who had been in her employ. Intrigued, I set about finding out what I could regarding the tale. Though the legal detail of the allegation did not prove completely accurate, the vicious outcome did. With that revelation I was suddenly drawn in by the desire, the need to discover all that I could about my great-great-grandfather, Theodore Burmester, and his wife, Ariminta.

I have always been intrigued by the notion that our human paths seem to randomly cross space with one-another like intersecting vectors. Sometimes our paths cross without any knowledge that we have done so, as when two friends pass by within feet of each other on a crowded street or mall. Other times we may cross paths with a stranger and our lives are changed forever. I think it is even more fascinating to contemplate crossing time as well as space with other people and ancestors. For example, when holding one of my mother's coins from her collection with a date of 1814, I wonder whether James Madison or John Marshall or some other venerable American hero may have held that same coin as I now hold it. As I searched for the story of my family, I discovered that Theodore and I had crossed paths in time and space. I learned that he too had been a lawyer and in our younger lives each of us had walked across the Isthmus of Panama from the Atlantic to the Pacific.

Growing up in Utah was an experience unlike growing up anywhere else. Though my neighbors and childhood friends were always thoughtful and kind, there was always a gulf that separated us. Unlike them, I was not Mormon. It was for the most part nothing mean or hurtful. But it was undeniably evident that we were different. One of my earliest memories was the happiness I felt during Spring and Fall Conference for the Church of Jesus Christ of Latter-day Saints because my friends did not have to go to church all day and they would be available to play with me on Sunday. I also distinctly remember an occasion when an adult, I think a parent or a teacher, asked me my address which I told her. Because the address was unfamiliar, she asked, "What ward do you live in?" A "ward" is a house of worship in the Church of Jesus Christ of Latter-day Saints. If you are a Saint in Utah, you attend a specific "ward" based on where you live, like public school. I don't think this was some sneaky way of determining whether I was a Latter-day Saint or not, rather it gave her a better grasp of the general location of my home when I told her "Canyon Rim." In school, when we learned about state history, we had a few brief lessons on the indigenous peoples and the early transitory European visitors like trappers and Father Escalante. But the main focus of the class was the history of the Mormons. There was not even a token lesson about the Methodist Church in Utah that my family attended. We were taught nothing about non-Mormons in early Utah except that they continued to harass the Mormons who had fled from persecution in Illinois to the Great Salt Lake Valley. In high school, nearly all of my friends had "release time" in their class schedule which is simply a device for getting around separation of church and state prohibitions on teaching Mormon Seminary in public schools. So, each day my friends all shared this class in common where they would stroll off campus to the LDS Seminary building across the street.

There came a time when I began to look around me and see all the pink elephants and wonder to myself, "What in the world is going on? I am not one of them so why am I here?" I found that in pursuing the story of Theodore and Ariminta I came to understand why these children of German immigrants moved from their homes in Pennsylvania and Illinois to Oregon where their paths fatefully crossed and ultimately, why I came to be here in Zion.

What follows is the history that I uncovered through my search to find my family story. This is a history of both Theodore and Ariminta. One thing I learned along the way is that because of our patrilineal culture, we forget the history of our mothers. But I am just as much the son of Ariminta as I am the son of Theodore. Further, this book is a history not only of Theodore and Ariminta but also the paths that they took and the people, other vectors, with whom they intersected along the way. Those intersections, chance and planned encounters with other people altered the course they themselves were on, and as that course changed directions, hither and yon, it led them to me, here in Salt Lake City in the twenty-first century.

Theodore and Ariminta, Collection of the Author.

Chapter 1: Crossing the Isthmus

<u>Life in Philadelphia</u>

December 13, 1837, Albany, Ohio. Wilhelmina screamed out in agony as the contraction gripped her. Then as it released its hold on her she fell back on the bed and panted. Moments later, drenched in sweat from the exertion, the contraction struck again, and she cried out. When she went into labor, she and her husband, Henry Burmester, had been staying at the home of friends, a long way from their own home in Philadelphia, Pennsylvania. Nevertheless, she gave birth to a healthy baby boy the couple named Theodore. His mother, Wilhelmina Fredericka Josephina Heiner, was born in Württemburg in 1811, well before it became part of the modern nation of Germany. Her name suggests her parents paid proper homage to all of the important potentates of the two dominant kingdoms vying for supremacy over the German-speaking peoples. She had a wonderful voice and the gift to play nearly any musical instrument she could lay her hands on; and together with two of her sisters she conducted a women's musical seminary. Theodore's father, Henry, was born in Hamburg. Both Wilhelmina and Henry immigrated to Philadelphia, Pennsylvania, where they met, married and then made their home. Thus, it was only by accident that Theodore was not born in the "City of Brotherly Love" like his siblings.

By 1840, three years after Theodore was born, Philadelphia was on the cusp of the industrial revolution and during the course of that next decade it would lead the nation into radically altered social and economic arrangements. This had both positive and ill effects on the residents who grew in number from 258,037 in 1840 to 408,762 by the end of the decade.[1] Though the population increased by 58%, the number of dwellings increased by only 15%. The result was a city which was much more crowded and noisier than it had been, and whose residents were far more economically disparate. While the number of Philadelphia millionaires grew to five and those with fortunes over one hundred thousand dollars grew to 234, the new factories that gave them their wealth consolidated unskilled workers, male, female, and child alike into a system of faceless industrial serfdom. Under the old regime, a young man could count on enhancing his economic and social position through hard work as an apprentice under the tutelage of a master craftsman. Under the new industrial hierarchy, there was very little social or economic mobility for workers other than downward. In the factories, unskilled laborers earned an average of between 60 cents and 80 cents per day. Girls working in a match factory earned $2.50 per week. Economic dislocation resulted in homelessness for some, possibly as many as 5000.

Old neighborhoods slipped into slums while grand old homes in deteriorating neighborhoods were converted into cheap tenements. Three-story-high bandbox row houses lined back alleys

---

[1] This figure includes both city and county totals. Elizabeth M. Giffen, "Industrial Development and Social Crisis 1841-1854," *Philadelphia, A 300-Year History*, eds. Russell F. Weigley et. al., (New York: W. W. Norton and Co.), 340.

and courts providing one room, usually not much more than 100 square feet per floor. Rooms could be let for 12 ½ cents per day and sleeping space on the floor then sublet for 2 cents.

The streets themselves became dirtier and more crowded by decade's end as well. Hundreds of hacks (horse drawn carriages for hire) and horse drawn busses ranged through the streets in addition to private traffic. Although train locomotives were banned from the city because of the fire hazard they presented from sparks emitted from wood fired engines, the cargo cars were pulled through the streets ever so slowly by horses.

At night 1700 lamps fueled by underground gas lines illuminated many of the city's streets. The most impressive modern marvel however was indoor plumbing. 22,000 homes, roughly a third of all homes, were supplied with water. However, a mere six public baths and a number of public hydrant pumps supported everyone else.

All that water being pumped into houses and public baths had to go somewhere after being used, and that somewhere was the Schuylkill River. Nevertheless, if the upstream supply contained less solid waste than New York City's water supply, city fathers were content. Apparently downstream consumers were not their concern.

Epidemics occasionally erupted and with so many people concentrated in such a small space many people died—cholera killed 1012 in 1849, small pox killed 427 in 1852, followed by yellow fever in 1853 which took another 127. Every summer the residents had to contend with outbreaks of typhus, dysentery, and malaria, each of which killed hundreds more. Of course, tuberculosis was ever constant. Nevertheless, the mortality rate in Philadelphia during the 1840s declined slightly even while the mortality rates in other large American cities were rising.

This was the world in which Theodore grew up. Henry and Wilhelmina had six children, three daughters Anna Maria, Catherine Louise, and Mary, and three sons including Theodore, William and young Henry junior.[2] German immigrants to Philadelphia were the earliest immigrant group and thereby had it a little better than other groups like the Irish or Africans who followed them. Germans had better jobs, two-thirds worked in the trades like tailoring, shoemaking and baking.[3] Henry, the father, was a clerk trained in accounting. He worked for a large hardware company and made a decent living. But in 1849, when gold was discovered at Sutter's Mill, men's expectations changed dramatically. It created a unique opportunity to escape from a lifetime of servitude in a company where there was little hope for advancement. There were now fortunes to be made out west and the already rich were not immune from its siren call.

The hardware company knew that if there were men getting rich from extracting gold from the earth in California Territory then those men would need tools and supplies. The company decided sometime in 1852 that it would send Henry out

---

[2] A seventh child, the couple's first born, died within a year of birth.
[3] http://www2.hsp.org/exhibits/Balch%20resources/phila_ellis_island.html.

to San Francisco to set up and run a new warehouse.[4] Henry felt honored by the company placing their confidence in him after eighteen years of dedicated service. So, he left behind his very substantial family and set sail for California and the promise of riches beyond their previous imagination.

In 1852 there were three ways to get from Philadelphia to San Francisco. One could place what ever they could carry in a wagon, on a horse, or on their own back and walk there. This method took about a year and was very dangerous. If hostile indigenous people didn't get you, starvation, disease, injury or bad weather often did. The second method was to book passage onboard a sailing vessel and sail south to nearly the Antarctic, through the Straits of Magellan, around what is now Argentina and up the west coast of South America and Central America. This too took nearly a year, was expensive and very dangerous even after the discovery of the passage through the Straits. The third option was to sail to a new nation called New Grenada in what is present-day Panama, traverse the Isthmus by foot, and obtain passage on another ship from Panama City on the Pacific Coast to San Francisco. This route was much quicker than either of the other two methods and less expensive. Traveling from New York to San Francisco by the Panama route shortened the trip to 5,000 sailing miles from the 13,000 the same trip took to go around the Horn of

---

[4] Carla Burmester, Theodore's daughter, does not identify the name of the company.

South America.[5] The one drawback to the Panama route was that though it was a mere fifty miles across the Isthmus, it was among the most hot, humid, disease-infested stretches of land anywhere on the earth.

It is unclear which route Henry took from Philadelphia to California, only that he went by ship. There are several varying accounts on the rest of the family. One point upon which all sources agree is that Theodore crossed the Isthmus of Panama on foot. One account, that of Theodore's youngest brother, little Henry, claims that the rest of the family followed their father to California "the following year by way of the Isthmus of Panama." Two of Theodore's children claim Theodore and his brother William alone crossed the Isthmus. One states "Theodore and William ran away to California in 1850 after William had flattened his schoolteacher with a lead inkwell, knocking him unconscious and causing both boys to think they had killed him. He suffered no ill effects however. They worked passage to Panama aboard ship, crossed the Isthmus on foot and made the trip to San Francisco on a sailing vessel."

Although the date is not precisely accurate, the rest of the story is hinted at by another account in which Theodore's daughter, Wilma Bishop, tells her correspondent that the family's trek from Philadelphia to Oregon via San Francisco "is another

---

[5] David McCullough, *The Path Between the Seas: The Creation of the Panama Canal 1870-1917*, (New York: Simon and Schuster, 1977), 34.

story but full of interest." In any event she too confirms that Theodore crossed the Isthmus on foot.

<u>The Isthmus of Panama Route</u>

Once Ferdinand Magellan discovered the route around the Cape Horn, other enterprising men set about looking for an even faster and less expensive way to get from the Atlantic Coast of North America or from Europe to the American Pacific coastal territories or the Orient. Expeditions surveyed different potential routes across the continental divide in what are now called Panama and Nicaragua. As a possible site for a wagon-capable road or rail line, the Isthmus of Panama offered one distinct advantage over all others: it was the narrowest point on the land bridge between the great Northern and Southern Continents. As case in point, in 1670 the famous pirate Henry Morgan successfully led his men through the jungle to sack Fort San Larenzo at the mouth of the Chagres River and then across the Isthmus where he and his men burned Panama City. Nevertheless, the great pirate's feats notwithstanding, most knowledgeable people considered the jungle impenetrable.

In 1845 there was no wagon trail anywhere across the Isthmus much less a railroad. That year a tireless thinker and merchant named William Henry Aspenwall acquired the government contract for ocean mail service between Panama and Oregon Territory. Conventional entrepreneurs thought he was nuts, after all there were no great ports, no industry, no coal for steamships, and no repair yards.[6] The following year, acting on his own initiative and not the behest of anyone, the American chargé d'affairs, Benjamin Alden Bidlack, signed a treaty for the United States with the government of New Grenada guaranteeing to the United States the exclusive right of transit across the Isthmus of Panama.[7] The rights and obligations he secured for his country did not generate an abundance of excitement back home in the United States. Indeed, Bidlack's Treaty, his only claim to fame, was not ratified by the Senate until the summer of 1848, a year and a half after he signed it, and then only after New Grenada's special envoy lobbied hard for the treaty. Sadly, Bidlack never got to see what William Aspenwall would do with his treaty, for he died just seven months after the Senate ratified it.

Of course, part of Aspenwall's genius was that he just happened to obtain the contract, and incorporate his new Pacific Mail Steamship Company (PMSS Co.) just at the moment James Marshall discovered gold in the American River while erecting John Sutter's new sawmill.[8] Initially, Aspenwall obtained the steamship, California, which was available for service in San Francisco in February 1848. The SS California was soon joined by the steamships Panama and Oregon. In addition to Aspenwall's service on the Pacific side, George Law's United States Mail

---

[6] http://web.archive.org/web/20061113105153/http://www.eraoftheclipperships.com/page62.html.

[7] McCullough, *The Path Between the Seas*, 32.

[8] Gold discovered January 1848; PMSS Co. incorporated in New York April 12, 1848.

Steamship Company obtained the contract for service to the Atlantic side. Together, the two federally authorized mail shipping companies easily met the suddenly strong demand for travel to and from Panama. However, a bottleneck formed as a consequence of the 50-mile walk across the Isthmus. Aspenwall together with partners commissioned a survey for a rail line to run from Fort San Lorenzo to Panama City.[9] In April 1850 with their report in hand, Aspenwall and his partners, John Stephens and Henry Chauncy incorporated the Panama Railroad Company.

The company began work in May 1850 but immediately ran into problems. First, George Law purchased the land around Fort San Lorenzo and Porto Bello and demanded stock in the new rail company.[10] Undeterred, Aspenwall changed his start point to a swampy island called Manzanillo in Navy (Limon) Bay. Engineers dropped thousands of tons of rocks into the swamp. After a year the tracks stretched a mere two miles to a small ridge called monkey hill, named for all the screaming monkeys living there. These monkeys, called howler monkeys, make a horrific racket completely out of proportion to their diminutive stature.

The next task required the engineers to span a three-mile quicksand swamp. On and on it went, mile after torturous mile. What engineers had planned to take two years to build, ended up taking them five, at a cost of eight million dollars, six times the

---

[9] John Haskell Kemble, *The Panama Route: 1848-1869*, (Columbia: University of South Carolina Press, 1990), 179.
[10] http://web.archive.org/web/20061113105153/http://www.eraoftheclipperships.com/page62.html.

projected figure. The human cost was even more staggering. The company did not keep records, so no one knows with any degree of certainty how many laborers died. Legend has it that 74,000 died, one for each tie laid. Historian David McCullough suggests a more reasonable figure is between six and twelve thousand mostly unknown laborers died miserable deaths from cholera, dysentery, yellow fever, and small pox.[11] Moreover, in the seemingly bottomless swamp where the company spent the majority of two years, they had no dry place to burry these nameless beings when they died. Then, adding insult to injury, apparently in an attempt to squeeze every last penny out of these poor wretched men they placed their corpses into barrels and pickled them for convenient shipping to medical schools and hospitals the world over. The railroad continued its morbid trade in corpses, eventually earning enough money to fund a small hospital in the Atlantic coastal town of Colón.[12]

But before there was a railroad there was still a demand to cross the Isthmus on foot. On January 7, 1849, the first trekkers hit the beach at the mouth of the Chagres River just below the silent gaze of the ruins of Fort San Lorenzo perched high upon the cliffs above them. Completely ill-prepared for what lay immediately before them, a trek across 50 or 60 miles of hot humid jungle, 200 North American men dressed predominantly in long-sleeve red flannel shirts carrying everything on their backs that they needed

---

[11] McCullough, *The Path Between the Seas*, 37.
[12] Ibid.

to start their new life in California stepped off the ship. The trekkers had no idea what direction they needed to go and the indigenous people they first encountered must have thought them a strange sight. The two groups could not understand one another despite the North Americans yelling louder and louder in a vain attempt to convey their questions. Nevertheless, all two hundred successfully completed the trip to Panama City, albeit hollow-eyed and caked with mud when they stumbled out of the jungle.[13]

Hundreds of treks ensued, and an American village of Chagres grew out of the jungle at the base on the right bank of the river, opposite the native village already there.[14] Indigenous people hired out canoe rides up the Chagres. Their canoes, called "bungos" were carved from logs, twenty to twenty-five feet in length and up to three feet in width. Three to four natives would pole the canoe with two to four passengers up the shallows of the river, which, depending on the skill of the native crew, took three to four days. Then Lieutenant Ulysses S. Grant made the trip in 1852 and later described naked natives walking the length of the boat on planks wide enough to walk attached to the outside of the boat pressing their shoulders into poles and thus propelling the boat of 30 to 40 passengers up river 1 to 1.5 miles per hour.[15] Trekkers spent evenings in native huts in villages along the way. But by 1853 hotels and saloons had sprung up in the terminal river

---

[13] Ibid, 33.

[14] Kemble, *The Panama Route*, 167.

[15] Ulysses S. Grant, *Personal Memoirs of U. S. Grant*, (New York: Literary Classics of the United States, Inc., 1990), 131.

towns of Cruces and Gorgona. The terminal point of the river traffic changed during dry season (December to April) from the former to the latter, four-and-one-half miles downstream. After debarkation from the canoe, the traveler made the last twenty to twenty-five miles on foot or mule-back through jungle trails barely three feet wide.

It was a difficult journey. They could not depend on finding or purchasing food along the way, and so had to carry what they could. The jungle heat and inadequate support quickly weakened the trekkers making them vulnerable to the same diseases that afflicted the railroad workers. Many, sick with cholera or Chagres fever, were unable to take another step and died right there on the side of the trail. Mules too suffered, especially during rainy season (May to December) when the trails devolved into a gooey morass; their carcasses lined the trail half buried in the deep-brown mud.

The SS Tennessee

The first three ships William Aspenwall brought into service for the PMSS Co. were roughly the same in capacity.[16] The California, Panama, and the Oregon were all wooden side-wheel steamers roughly 200 feet in length with two decks and three masts and weighed in at just under 1100 tons. In contrast, the Tennessee, unlike her original three sisters, was not built for service in the Pacific for the PMSS Co. Aspenwall purchased the

---

[16] Kemble, *The Panama Route*, 39.

Tennessee from the Savannah Steam Navigation Company in December 1849 where she had serviced the New York to Savannah traffic. More to the point, while the Tennessee was like her sister ships a wooden side-wheel steamer with two decks and three masts, she was significantly bigger, 211 feet long and over 1200 tons. When she first entered the Bay of Panama enroute from her former duty on the Eastern seaboard the local paper wrote:

> [T]his great leviathan of the Pacific came careening up in majestic style towards the anchorage of the Bay of Panama, and as she neared the place of mooring, the batture was lined with smiling countenances and sparkling eyes and stalwart arms, all to join in the loud huzza...[17]

Although passenger service aboard the Tennessee was highly thought of by passengers at the time, it was a far cry from the luxurious accommodations of cruise liners that transit the Panama Canal today. First, there were no refrigerators or freezers and consequently all ships carried livestock (cattle, sheep, hogs, and poultry) for slaughter during the voyage for fresh meat. There were typically three levels of accommodations for passengers. First-class consisted of staterooms that were furnished with between two and four berths one on top of the other, carpeted floors, mirror, toilet stand, wash bowl, water bottles and glasses. Second-class entitled the passenger to the same decks and services that first-class passengers enjoyed, however the passenger slept in a berth curtained from the many other passengers who shared that

---

[17] Ibid, 39-40.

same room. Steerage was a completely different experience altogether. There were no curtains, or rooms for that matter, that separated passengers in steerage. Rather, the entire bay was open and filled with racks of sleeping berths. Commonly there was no segregation of quarters for men, women, and children. Indeed, when there was segregation it was so unusual that it was reported in the newspapers. In steerage, each sleeping space was approximately six feet long and 18 inches wide, and 24 inches separated a bunk from the one above it (or the deck in the case of top berths). The berths were arranged in threes so that the person sleeping in the middle berth could only get to their bed by way of one of the two outside berths.

On the morning of February 1, 1853, the SS Tennessee churned its way out of San Francisco harbor for its second run of the year down the Pacific Coast to Panama City.[18] Fourteen days later, on the fifteenth, at 5:00 o'clock in the afternoon she paddled past the Pearl Islands in the Bay of Panama to the dock in Panama City. There she moored, and took on passengers, baggage, supplies, and mail for the return trip. On the morning of February 19, the SS Tennessee steamed out of the Bay of Panama for the last time.

The Tennessee stopped for supplies in Acapulco on February 28 and from that point on pursued the same basic route

---

[18] https://www.maritimeheritage.org/passengers/tn030653.html. The wreck of the Tennessee is noted also in Kemble, *The Panama Route*, at 248. All details on the last voyage of the SS Tennessee are taken from The Maritime Heritage Project reprints from the Daily Alta California.

within a few hours time of two other steamships: Pacific and Cortes. The Tennessee left just after noon on March 1, three hours after the Pacific and one hour before the Cortes. On March 5, she passed the Pacific.

That night a thick fog set in, shrouding the entire San Francisco Bay coastline. Maritime navigation at this time was more of an art than science. With no radar, sonar, or global positioning satellites the nineteenth-century mariner aided by compass and charts had to identify stellar constellations or important landmarks to be certain of his location. Otherwise, he resorted to dead reckoning, a technique of calculating one's position based on time, speed, and heading from the last known position.

Because of the fog, Captain Mellus was forced to use dead reckoning to Mile Rock, a prominent landmark near the mouth of the San Francisco Bay. To make sure that they did not run aground his crew used a measured rope with weights at the end to measure the water's depth as they approached, getting readings of six and seven fathoms. Soon someone spotted land which Mellus believed was the South Head, the southern jaw of the open mouth of San Francisco Bay. Mellus immediately ordered more steam let on, but then quickly realized that the land the lookout had spotted was not the South Head at all. Another crew member called out that there was a high ledge of rocks immediately astern. By this time Mellus could see that he had maneuvered his ship into a small cove, and with a ledge of rocks behind him, he could not back out. Mellus ordered the ship ahead to gain room in which to turn around. But before he had gained that room the crew and passengers felt a sudden halting jerk and heard the terrible scrape as the bottom aft hung up on rocks. Before Mellus could issue any further orders to free the Tennessee, she swung around and went aground on the beach broadside.

Captain Mellus ordered the Chief Mate, Mr. Dowling, to leap over the side of the ship to the shore where they tossed him a hawser, or rope, that they could use to move the ship if they received assistance or with which they could secure the ship from further wave damage. Very quickly the crew learned that they had entered Indian Cove and were in fact a little more than four miles north of the entrance to the San Francisco Bay.

Once the ship was secure the crew evacuated the passengers and mail from the ship and set them up into the grassy cove. They erected tents for the passengers while they awaited assistance, still holding out hope that with help they might yet pull the leviathan from her sandy perch.

Throughout the night the waves continued to roll in and out. Though the ship was tied down, each wave lifted her up four to five feet and then as the wave ran back out the ship crashed back down onto the sandy beach. When first light came, the Steam Ships Goliah and Thomas Hunt, which had come to Tennessee's aid, were seen just offshore but alas, it was too late. In the gathering light it was plain for all to see that the SS Tennessee had suffered greatly from the repeated crashing, her back was fatally broken.

The crew set about off-loading furniture, passengers' baggage and finally the ship's goods and stores, all of which was safely on shore by 2:00 o'clock in the afternoon. Steamship Confidence joined Goliah and both sent boats into shore to retrieve passengers for the trip back down the coast to San Francisco. Although the seas were rough, Mr. Isaacs, SS Tennessee's purser, reported that all of the passengers, their baggage and the mail (200 bags worth) were loaded aboard the two rescue ships within four hours and yet no one was hurt, nor any property lost.

All the passengers and newspapers reporting the loss of the Tennessee seemed acutely aware that Captain Mellus and his crew were in serious trouble with the Pacific Mail Steamship Company. The subject of several articles reported in the Daily Alta California asserted the professional competence, notwithstanding the wreck, of the captain and his crew. Different groups of passengers demanded publication of their commendation of specific crew members for their performance immediately following the ship's running aground. One such Complimentary Card published March 9, 1853 in the Daily Alta California complimented the Boatswain.

> "We, passengers by the steamer
> Tennessee, do hereby present our compliments to
> Mr. George Robbins, Boatswain up on said vessel,
> for his untiring exertions in securing the landing

of passengers, baggage, and mail from the boat to the beach where she stranded."[19]

Fifty-five passengers signed the card complimenting Mr. Robbins. Among those names is the signature: "T. Burmester."

<u>Was Theodore Burmester Aboard the SS Tennessee?</u>

Is it possible that Theodore Burmester, son of Henry and Wilhelmina, was aboard the Steamship Tennessee when she ran aground in the early morning hours of March 6, 1853? There is no mention of it by any of the children who later told the dutiful Latter-day Saint genealogy researcher what happened to Theodore and William. Nor is it mentioned in a newspaper interview of Theodore's younger brother Henry written years later. The report of the complimentary card in the Daily Alta California does not give any more precise identification or details of the signatory other than "T. Burmester."

Nevertheless, the name Burmester is somewhat unusual and "T. Burmester" even more so. Moreover, the SS Tennessee incident occurs precisely when the trip was to have been made. Though letters written by Theodore's children, Hank Burmester and Wilma Bishop, do not mention the grounding of the Tennessee, they were written many years later, indeed when they were old, and the actual participants were long dead. The stories were mere highlights that came to their minds as they replied to the distant relative's requests for information; they were not

---

[19] https://www.maritimeheritage.org/passengers/tnwreck.html.

thoughtful responses to systematic examination by a professional researcher. The article about young Henry is an edited article with limited space.

The manifest is unfortunately of little help. Only 22 of the 55 names on the Complimentary Card are clearly found in the manifest. Another nine are reasonably similar to conclude that they are the same persons. Thus, 24 names from the Complimentary Card, including "T. Burmester," are not found on the manifest. Of interesting note however, is a lone entry in the typed manifest found on the Maritime Heritage Project website for an "A. Barmester" aboard the ill-fated Tennessee. Theodore's oldest sister was named Anna. The original manifest was almost certainly handwritten and subsequently transcribed.

Just because the grounding of the SS Tennessee is not mentioned in the documents in my possession does not mean that Theodore was not aboard on March 6, 1853. For example, Lloyd S. Thompson, Theodore's great-nephew (his brother William's grandson) in a similar responsive letter did not mention walking across the Isthmus, though it is a certainty that he did. Thus, it seems entirely possible that Theodore was aboard the SS Tennessee on her final voyage.

If one looks at a map of the California coastline today there is no longer an "Indian Cove" four miles north of San Francisco Bay. Indian Cove is known today as "Tennessee Cove" for the proud steamship whose back was broken as it lay stranded on that beach in March 1853.

To Oregon

Once Theodore and his family arrived in San Francisco they learned that the warehouse which Henry had been sent to operate no longer existed. It had been consumed in one of several major fires that struck the city between 1849 and 1855. Faced with the choice of returning to Philadelphia or finding something else out west, Theodore's father elected to pursue the latter. So, once they were reunited in 1853, he moved his family to Bilyeu Den in Linn County, Oregon Territory.

Chapter 2: The Mothers' Stories

Ariminta was, like Theodore, born of German stock. However, her ancestors immigrated to North America as religious refugees before there was a United States. Hartman Hunsaker was a "Dunkard"[20] or Old German Baptist Brethren, so called because of their emphasis on public full immersion baptism in local lakes and streams. Soon after their founding in 1708 most of the Brethren began to flee their German homeland to Pennsylvania and New Jersey colonies.[21] Seeking religious freedom he arrived in Philadelphia on September 10, 1731, with his wife and several young children including three-year-old John. At first the family settled in Germantown. As an adult John moved his family west, settling for periods in Lancaster Pennsylvania, and what would become Kentucky.

In 1841, John's great-grandson, Jacob T. Hunsaker, at twenty-four years of age moved his family to Adams County Illinois. His wife, Emily Collings, twenty-two years, was pregnant with their third child.[22] They lived humbly yet typically for young couples on the western frontier.

---

[20] Q. Maurice Hunsaker & Gwen Hunsaker Haws, eds., *History of Abraham Hunsaker and His Family*, (Salt Lake City: Hunsaker Family Organization, 1957), 4.

[21] Donald B. Kraybill and Carl F. Bowman, *On the Backroad to Heaven: Old Order Hutterites, Mennonites, Amish, and Brethren*, (Baltimore: Johns Hopkins University Press, 2001), 137. Blending pietism and Anabaptism the Christian separatists reject modern culture and attempt to live the New Testament strictly.

[22] Marianne D'Arcy, "Reminiscences," (unpublished Memoir 1900), ed. Daisy Sanford, University of Oregon Special Collections.

Upon arrival at their new homestead their top priority was shelter. To meet that need they built a one-room log cabin with a stone hearth for cooking and providing heat in the winter. The second priority was food. Accordingly, they soon planted crops. Further down on the necessaries list were clothing and cash. Emily contributed on these accounts by spinning yarn and knitting socks and then selling any excess beyond her family's needs.

By the time winter set in Jacob and Emily had built their one-room cabin, complete with four walls, a roof and stone fireplace. However, though they enjoyed four walls and a roof, Jacob had not had the time to chink (plaster the cracks between the logs with clay) the walls before winter wrapped the cabin in its icy tendrils. Thus, the cabin remained drafty and exceedingly cold throughout that first winter. By New Year's Day it was bitterly cold. When Jacob woke up on the first morning of 1842, he rolled over to Emily and gave the customary light-hearted greeting, "New Year's Gift, Emily."

Emily replied neither light-hearted nor alarmed, but rather, matter-of-factly, "New Year's Gift to you Jacob, but you better get up quickly, rake out the coals and get a fire going, because I think you will truly have a New Year's Gift today!"

Jacob quickly pulled back the covers and sat up. His two children, Horton, three, and Josephine, one and a half, lay asleep on a trundle bed. He first climbed carefully out of bed to the cold dirt floor and then hastily pushed the trundle bed back underneath his bed so that he could more easily move. He stoked the fire and dressed. Once the fire glowed brightly Jacob ran out the door to the nearby home of a neighbor skilled in the art of childbirth whom they affectionately called Grandmother Stewart.

Emily was accurate in her prediction. Marianne, named for Jacob's beloved blind sister, was born on that cold New Year's Day in 1842. Jacob and Emily's family continued to live in this same cabin for another four years and during that time Grandma Stewart helped Emily give birth two more times.

The next child born after Marianne was Ariminta, born April 28, 1843. During the cold months Jacob suffered from "lung fevers," and during those times the children had to tend to themselves, as Emily did nearly all the chores. One chilly November morning Emily was outside milking a cow, Marianne, not yet two years old, had to watch over her baby sister in the cabin while Jacob lay on the bed incapacitated with "lung fever."

Minti, as Ariminta was then called, could not yet walk but was adept at standing and could reach out and grab things with her tiny hands. Minti stood shakily and reached out to the coffee pot that was heating on the hearth and pulled it to her. The pot tipped over with a clang, pouring hot coffee on Minti's little legs and feet. Minti suddenly screamed out with pain. Josephine ran across the room and swept Minti up and set her on the bed next to their father.

Jacob gasped weakly, "Mary, get your mother!"

Marianne, startled from her temporary stupor, ran out the door yelling, "Mother! Mother! Minti burned herself. Father says to come at once!"

Emily stood up immediately. Then quickly grasping Mary's urgent call she set the bucket full of milk down and ran to the cabin, leaving Marianne crying because she had been forgotten. Though certainly painful, the scalding Ariminta suffered did not apparently leave any lasting effects.

The Storm

When Marianne was about three years old, she was allowed to go to school with Horton and Josephine (Ariminta was still only about eighteen months old). One morning Marianne sat with Jake Abbott, a neighbor boy of the same age. Suddenly the sky grew very dark with yellow-green clouds and the teacher, a very young woman, looked out the window with great alarm. Though she was young she was old enough to know what dangers the sudden appearance of such dark clouds portended. She was terrified.

She abruptly stopped talking to the children and walked hurriedly to the door. She looked up at the sky as the students spoke with one-another in hushed tones—fear now growing in them more from their teacher's strange behavior than from the dark clouds. The teacher turned back into the room and told the students to grab their things and go home. "Do not play, do not dawdle, just run home to your parents! Now go!"

Once outside the wind was blowing sticks and leaves and it was difficult to hear. All the children knew the path through the woods by heart. Nevertheless, Horton ordered Jake Abbott to follow close and Marianne to do the same behind Jake.

"Josephine, you bring up the tail," Horton said. "You are the oldest. You must make sure that Mary and Jake do not get lost."

The four little children ran and plunged into the woods in a line. The wind grew stronger until it was a roaring fury while the sky dimmed nearly as dark as night. Great branches broke off with a crack so loud it pierced the roar of the wind. Horton stumbled into bushes with thick limbs where none had been before. For a moment he thought he was lost until he realized that their path was blocked by shorn branches. Horton clambered through the downed limbs and Josephine helped the two younger children through the obstacles. The children set off again in a chain down the forest path. In the darkness Marianne tripped and fell on another branch. Josephine quickly bent down and helped her sister to her feet and off they went.

Horton led them through the woods until they emerged from its dark cover. Though the forest trees gave way to open fields the storm clouds still shrouded the land in an eerie gloom. The frightened children were relieved to see through the false dusk Jacob and Mr. Abbott running to their rescue. Jacob and Mr. Abbott swept the youngest ones into their arms and called for Josephine and Horton to follow. Suddenly warmed and relieved from the overwhelming stress, Marianne fell asleep in her father's arms before they even reached their home.

Pigeon Creek

In January 1845, Jacob left his young family including his pregnant wife to go tend to his ailing father. "Grandfather Hunsaker" died on the 27th of January and while Jacob was gone Emily gave birth to her fifth child, whom they named Jacob, a little towhead boy.

Later, after the elder Jacob returned, the family prepared to visit Emily's parents one Sunday morning. Emily had the baby and the girls, Josephine, Marianne, and Ariminta, ready and dressed in their nice dresses before Horton and Jacob had even finished their chores.

Jacob told Emily, "Go on ahead. Horton and I'll catch up as soon as I shave, and Horton gets dressed."

So, the ladies and baby Jacob, "Little Red Bird" as the girls called him, left.[23] Along the way they had to cross Pigeon Creek. However, when they reached the ford the creek was still frozen. Not knowing how thick the ice was Emily was afraid to cross. Contemplating whether she should even make the attempt, she paced up and down the near shore holding the baby in her arms looking for a place to cross. Finally, she told the little girls, "Wait here. I am going to cross and see if the ice will hold."

---

[23] Marianne D'Arcy claims they gave him that name "because he was always in a red dress." D'Arcy, "Reminiscences."

Slowly, nervously, she stepped one foot, and paused. She then repeated this tentative advance alternating each foot and pausing as she crossed the ice. Breathlessly her daughters watched, when suddenly Emily, still holding "Little Red Bird" broke through the ice.

Mary and Minti screamed. Josephine saw that although their mother lost her breath for a moment because the water running underneath the surface of the ice was so cold, she still had the baby securely in her arms and the water was only just deeper than her knees. Josephine put her arms around her little sisters and finally quieted them. However, Emily could not get back out, for each time she tried to climb out the ice broke away. Though Josephine quieted their screaming, Mary and Minti continued to cry. Emily reassured them, calling out from the river, "Don't cry my little ones. Father will be along soon you will see."

Emily struggled for a few more minutes before they finally heard a wagon approaching. Hoping for the arrival of Jacob and Horton, they watched in anticipation. However, instead of Jacob and Horton it was Mr. Lyle, a neighbor, who crested the hill. The gentleman quickly recognized Emily's dire predicament and pulled his wagon to a stop when he reached them. He leaped down and without a word went out on the ice and helped Emily and baby Jacob back to the near bank where they were greeted by the much-relieved young girls.

Emily was soaked to her thighs and knew immediately that she could no longer make the trip to her parents' home in that condition. She quieted her daughters' gleeful chants and once she had their attention said, "Let's go home."

Once again Mary and Minti began to wail, this time in disappointment. "Oh Mother, we want to go to Grandmother's house," they cried.

"I cannot go like this she exclaimed," gesturing with her one free arm toward her soaking dress, steam rising in the cold air.

Just then Jacob and Horton appeared strolling over the hill. When Jacob saw what had just occurred, he agreed with Emily that they could not continue on with her soaking wet and the temperature so cold. Jacob silenced the girls' complaining and the family walked back home together.

The Oregon Trail

One day in late winter of 1845 Marianne sat on the floor near the fireplace. A fire burned steadily in the now chinked cabin, keeping it toasty warm despite the cold weather. Split wood lay neatly stacked in a pile next to the fireplace. Jacob sat on the bed holding baby Jacob. Emily was busy spinning yarn, and as she worked, she and Jacob discussed the merits of moving to Oregon Territory. They had engaged in several of these conversations, which took on a more urgent tenor when at moments such as this Jacob suffered from "lung fever."

Marianne, although now familiar with the term "Oregon" did not understand its meaning. "Father, what is Oregon?" she interrupted.

"Why child, Oregon is a country, a place, a long way from here, where we want to move to by and by," he replied.

"Which way is it?"

"Oh, that way," he said pointing west across the room in the direction of the fireplace.

Marianne followed his finger and saw Oregon: the fireplace. Later, Marianne was outside playing with her sisters, Josephine and Ariminta. Marianne taunted her siblings with claims that she knew something they didn't know.

"What is that?" Josephine demanded.

"Father says that we are moving to Oregon," she replied confidently.

"Where is Oregon?" Ariminta asked.

"That way," Marianne told her, pointing at the chimney.

"It is not!" Josephine interjected, knowing that Marianne had pointed back to their house, east of where they were playing.

"It is too. Father even said so," Marianne retorted.

"Oh you don't know," Josephine said. "Besides, I am not going anyway. I will run away first."

Despite Josephine's objections, the next year Jacob and Emily decided they would settle in Oregon. They began preparations—they would take two wagons, one drawn by their two horses, Cap, a big black stallion, and Dolly, a chestnut mare, and the other wagon drawn by oxen. They needed to collect food, lead, gunpowder and other essentials to make the long journey.

But they also had to get rid of everything that did not fit into the two wagons.

As they collected supplies and made other preparations, Josephine made it clear to all her family that she did not wish to leave their home in Illinois. She pleaded, pouted and stomped her feet but her parents were not moved. Josephine refused to give in. Finally, she shouted her stern warning, "I will not go, you shan't take me! I'll run away! You shan't take me!"

Despite her impassioned plea her parents largely ignored her cries, after all, she was still just a child, perhaps five or six years old. The family continued their preparations.

On the day they departed, friends and neighbors came around to bid them farewell. Jacob and two other young men took charge of the ox wagon and the several cows and other livestock they intended to herd along with them. Emily was to drive the smaller horse wagon. Everyone was hugging and crying and wishing the Hunsakers well. But as they prepared to leave, Emily realized Josephine was nowhere in sight.

The family began to search for Josephine, with friends and neighbors joining in. No one was particularly worried for her safety, suspecting it was another stunt to thwart their departure.

Emily's brother finally found her hiding on his farm. He alerted Jacob who came running. Jacob spoke gently to her, "Please come out daughter," (an endearing name he reserved exclusively for her) but she would not budge. Finally, he grabbed her by the waist and held her under one arm as he carried her back to the wagons. The whole time Josephine wriggled and kicked, crying that she did not want to go. Jacob gently placed her in Emily's wagon on a soft package of bedding. There she curled up face-down "sobbing pitifully." Emily rubbed her back and tried to comfort her. But she would not be consoled. Once they started, waving as they rolled away, Josephine crawled out and insisted on sitting on her mother's lap as they drove.

For two days the Hunsaker clan stopped at the homes of friends and relations as they made their way toward the jump-off point for the real trek. The stop at Grandfather Collings' home (Emily's father) was especially heart rending. "Oh Emily, Oh Emily, we will never see you again! Farewell," cried her loved ones. With only two exceptions they were correct.[24]

When Jacob's family finally departed the Collings' farm, Emily's brothers, George and James, and their dog, Tyler, accompanied them for several days. When George and James finally decided they had to return they gave Tyler to Horton.

Jacob led his family to Council Bluffs where they joined a wagon train forming to make the trip to Oregon. They formed a company and chose a captain to lead them. They checked loads and then prepared to cross the river.

Once they were finally ready, the girls were paddled across the Missouri River by Native Americans in a canoe. Emily

---

[24] During the rest of her life Emily was only visited in Oregon by two of her brothers, George and James. She herself never returned to Illinois. D'Arcy, "Reminiscences."

had each of the girls lie down in the bottom of the canoe, and then she sat in the bottom of the canoe holding baby Jake to her bosom. "Now close your eyes ladies and stay perfectly still. We do not want you to tip this canoe over and drown!"[25]

Meanwhile, Jacob and Horton worked with other men at the ferry site, loading wagons on board, tying them down, blind folding the horses. It took a long time to get the entire company across, but eventually they did.

Once across the Missouri the company made its way south and west toward the Platte River. The temperature climbed steadily as they crossed the prairie. Tyler and the children had to walk. The ground was so hot it burned the pads of poor old Tyler's feet. He began to whimper, and the children begged their mother to let Tyler ride in the wagon some of the time. On this issue at least, the children always got their way.

1846 was still early in the history of the Oregon Trail and Fort Kearney had not yet been established as a supporting base for the "Gateway to the Great Plains." Eventually, it would become the collection point for all trains regardless where they originated. Nevertheless, all trains converged at approximately that point along the Platte and indeed Hunsaker's train originating from Council Bluffs would soon be joined by a larger train that had left from St. Louis.

---

[25] D'Arcy, "Reminiscences."

At this second "jump-off" point the train made its first
contact with Native People in what the white settlers called
"Indian Country."[26] Early in the morning as their small train
loaded and prepared to depart, a small band of Native Americans
trotted up to the train on horseback. They signaled that they
wanted to talk to the leader of the white men, and the captain
stepped forward. The leader of the Native Band told the captain
that the white men should come no further. If they turned around
now and returned from whence they came, his people would spare
their lives. However, if the emigrants pressed ahead the leader of
the group promised that they would kill every last person before
they could get very far.

After only a brief consultation with some of the men that
were nearby, the captain told the Native American leader that they
would wait where they were for one day and decide what to do.
The leader scoffed with a dismissive grunt and the band rode off to
wait and watch.

The captain called for a council where he shared the
Natives American's ultimatum with the other members of the
train. The emigrants decided to put the choice to continue or to
turn around, to a vote. All adults voted, men and women. They all
knew that a much larger train was not far behind and that they
would almost certainly choose to continue. After some brief

---

[26] Marianne D'Arcy does not give the events of the crossing of the plains any
chronological order. Neither do the letters and other contributions of her sister,
Sarah, or her editor, Daisy Sanford. I have tried to sort them out as best I could
by inference, but in the end this sequence is my speculation.

discussion the group agreed "that they had started to Oregon, and to Oregon they would go—or die."[27]

The larger train arrived the next morning and the joint group of emigrants quickly organized a plan for how to proceed. The emigrants made sure each of the wagons had at least one or two well armed men on board. However, they agreed that the emigrants would not "start trouble." Instead, they would only respond if the Native warriors attacked them first. Jacob volunteered to lead the group out. He drove the smaller wagon pulled by the horses, Cap and Dolly so he exchanged places with Emily. The livestock were brought in close and the train started off.

At first, there were no indigenous people in sight. But soon they began to materialize from all directions as if they were springing forth from the earth itself. As they appeared, they ran straight toward the head of the train—Jacob's wagon.

The Native warriors formed a double row on either side of the wagons, a gauntlet, for them to pass through. Frequently a Native warrior would step out in front of Jacob's wagon and block his path until the horses were nearly on top of him, at which time he would finally step back out of the way.

The Native Americans did not say a word to the emigrants but kept up their gauntlet until around three o'clock in the

---

[27] D'Arcy, "Reminiscences." Quote purportedly came from a letter written by Sarah Hunsaker Tompkins, presumably added by editor, Sanford. The events were related to Sarah by her father, Jacob T. Hunsaker.

afternoon, Jacob judged by the sun. Throughout that time, the emigrants did not try to speak to the Native men confronting them, nor did the emigrants really speak to each other, they were so worried about their safety. The only words uttered during this silent drive through the gauntlet were the commands given to the horses and cattle. Then just as suddenly as they had appeared the warriors melted away. After that, the emigrants established a rotating guard watch when the train stopped each evening.

As they continued on their trek, each day seemed hotter to the travelers than the day before. With each step the emigrants grew more and more tired and tempers started to flare. One settler named Max Ramsey refused his shift at guard duty and others insisted that he take his turn. Mrs. Price scolded Ramsey for shirking his duty.

"Mr. Ramsey, if I wasn't a lady, I would tell you what I think of you!" she said sternly.

"Oh don't let that stop you, Mrs. Price," he shot back. It is not known whether Mrs. Price actually revealed her thoughts to Ramsey or whether Ramsey ever took his turn at guard duty.[28]

At night they stopped, the company circled their wagons, creating a corral to protect themselves from the great herds of buffalo and established the sentry, to provide early warning in case of raids by Native warriors or buffalo stampedes. Once the wagons were in place, Emily prepared dinner while Jacob and Horton

---

[28] D'Arcy, "Reminiscences."

helped the other men in the camp. Josephine helped her mother by looking after the little ones.

On one-night, Little Jacob, Jake, escaped from Josephine's watchful eye and wandered off and into the camp of several single men traveling together, whom the Hunsakers referred to as the "Bachelors." About the time Emily realized Jake was missing, she heard "shouts and laughter" erupting from the Bachelors' camp. Concerned, Emily walked toward the sound in hopes of finding her young son. Nearly halfway there she saw the toddler "carrying a big, smoking buffalo steak in his hand." The men laughed and explained how Jake had walked up to their frying pan and coolly helped himself to one of their steaks. The toddler brought the steak back to camp, half dragging it in the dirt, and plopped it onto a tin plate on the ground. There, he squatted down beside his prize, quite satisfied by his successful hunting trip.

Soon after the wagon train set out in earnest, a pattern of activity quickly developed each evening once they stopped and circled the wagons. Men, women and children had their own duties and responsibilities. The adults secured and cared for the animals, established security, and prepared evening meals. The children of the camp were sent out to search for and collect buffalo chips for fuel. A "penurious" bachelor named Waldo immediately joined the search and contested the children for the best and closest chips.

On one particular night Emily had only just begun preparing dinner when she saw a man race into camp on horseback yelling out a warning that a large herd of buffalo was stampeding in the direction of the camp. Immediately, Emily grabbed her children and placed them inside their wagon with her. Several men from the party retrieved rifles and raced out of camp on horseback toward the onrushing buffalo. They fired at the buffalo in the vanguard of the herd in an effort to redirect them. Meanwhile, the Hunsaker family huddled together in their wagon, terrified by the roar of the stampede combined with the sharp reports of men's rifles. Emily stared out the opening of the wagon wide-eyed. Suddenly, a massive black form leaped across the tongue of the wagon, next to the front opening and Emily reflexively lurched back from the opening and screamed.

For many minutes the family huddled together as the enormous herd thundered by as if one giant organism. Once the herd finally cleared the camp emigrants agreed they had been very fortunate to avoid any substantial loss from this near disaster. Indeed, not only had they avoided disaster, but the stampede resulted in a boon to the company as they feasted on buffalo steaks and tongue that night from the buffalo killed when the men first tried to divert the leading animals.

One day, as Emily drove the small wagon, Waldo rode up beside her and asked, "Mrs. Hunsaker, could you let me have just one match? I do want a smoke so much and mine are all back in the wagons."[29] Waldo had hired men to care for his wagons while

---

[29] Ibid.

he rode on horseback. Apparently, he frequently found himself separated from his wagons during the course of the march. Emily considered Waldo's request. Even though matches were a fairly dear commodity, it was only one match. So, she reached back into the wagon and retrieved one for him. This practice continued for several days, until finally Emily refused, apologizing to the man many had taken to calling "Old Maid Waldo" that unfortunately her matches were "back in the wagon…in the bottom of a deep box that she could not get into without stopping the wagon and unpacking it."

After the children had all eaten, Emily put the youngest children to bed and Horton helped his mother clean up. This journey was transformative for Horton. During this trek, he grew into a responsible young man. It also created a very close bond between mother and son. At times he would comfort her when she grieved the family she left behind.

Once the children were in bed, Emily gathered up their clothes and washed them when water was available so that they would have fresh clothes each morning.[30] Old Maid Waldo came by the Hunsaker camp one evening as Emily was washing clothes and begged her to wash just one shirt for him. She agreed to do so and Waldo, whose wagons were stocked with goods to establish a store in Oregon, promised, "You shall have a nice calico dress, as soon as I unpack my goods." In Oregon years later, Emily and

---

[30] Much of the first third of the journey (up to Independence Rock) paralleled the Platte River.

many other women on that same trip often shared a good laugh as they reminisced about the "nice calico dress" Old Maid Waldo had promised each of them but never delivered.

One of the emigrants became very ill and his wife, very concerned about his condition, came to a group who had clustered together for the night. They determined the man needed some brandy or whiskey for its medicinal value, but the woman did not have any. She asked Old Maid Waldo for a drop of whiskey or brandy from his stores. But Waldo replied that he was "Sorry but he didn't have a drop, as that was one of the things he had neglected to lay in."[31] Before Waldo finished his sorrowful explanation several other emigrants had run to their family wagons and returned with bottles of whiskey for the ailing man.

After paralleling the Platte River for nearly the entire length of the present state of Nebraska the emigrants came to the point in the trail where they had to cross the river. This was no small undertaking, and the train suffered its share of mishaps. The Hunsaker's ox wagon tipped over. Then as the children were being ferried across, Marianne's friend, Ann Doane, gave her a playful push and Marianne fell into the river. Buoyed by her dress and petticoats she floated swiftly down river until a man caught her downstream and retrieved her.[32]

---

[31] D'Arcy, "Reminiscences." Marianne D'Arcy does not tell us who the sick man was or who came to ask for help, just that "someone" did.

[32] In "Reminiscences," Marianne was not certain that this occurred on the Platte. However, in a 1928 Newspaper article, entitled "Mrs. Marianne D'Arcy, 86,

45 / Finding Theodore and Ariminta

When it was Old Maid Waldo's turn for his wagons to cross, he stood by and watched as one of his wagons also tipped over. After righting the wagon and pulling it up on the riverbank Waldo was mortified to see a dark liquid draining out the bottom of the wagon. Waldo ran up to the wagon and cried out in his high-pitched voice, "Oh, boys! Boys! Come quick, here is all my nice brandy that I paid five dollars a gallon for in St. Louis, broken and running out." Without even recognizing he had given away his lie about not having any brandy to share, Waldo greedily cupped his hands and held them under the brown liquid stream pouring out between the wagon floor boards. He brought it to his lips and drank a mouthful. Within seconds he spit the liquid back out—his whiskey bottles had not broken, rather the water had soaked his supply of homemade soap he had hidden on board. This too was an embarrassing revelation; fore Waldo had borrowed soap from many others on the pretence that he had none.

Eventually the train of emigrants made it across the Platte River.[33] The train rode north to the North Fork and then began to parallel that great branch of the river westward. They passed Chimney Rock which signaled to the company that they had made one-third of the distance. Unfortunately, most had no idea how much more difficult the terrain would be in the last two-thirds than the terrain they had just covered. As they followed the North Platte

---

Touched Lightly By Years," she asserts it was the Platte. I have a photocopy of this article, but I have not been able to find the source.

[33] Although D'Arcy talks about crossing the Platte, it appears she is really talking about the South Fork.

into present day Wyoming the trek became hotter and dryer. Soon the children complained of thirst incessantly, but due to strict rationing their desire remained unsatisfied. Poor Tyler too began to whimper and cry favoring paws that were burning in the hot soil. The children begged to allow Tyler to ride and Emily agreed to allow the dog to ride in her wagon.

As they pushed their way into present day Wyoming, Jacob and some of the other men noticed that another party of indigenous people was following them. That evening the men shared their concerns about the Native Americans they had seen following the wagon train. The Native Americans were camped so close that the emigrants could hear them all night long. The next day more indigenous people appeared and joined in following the train. At times the Native Americans riding on horseback came so close to the train that the emigrants could see their expressions of disapproval as they scowled at the emigrants and acted menacingly toward them.

After several days a Native American leader and his entourage trotted up on horseback to the wagon train which had stopped for the evening in coral style and demanded dinner for his band. The captain advised the emigrants that the best way to get past this latest confrontation with indigenous people was to give them their meal and move on.[34] Jacob was against it as he believed it would only encourage them. Besides the emigrants did not have

---

[34] "Mrs. Marianne D'Arcy, 86, Touched Lightly By Years."

extra food that they could just give away. The emigrants put the issue to a vote and the majority sided with the captain, so all the emigrants worked together to prepare a meal for their "visitors."

When the meal was prepared the emigrants laid out their pots and tin plates in a line on the ground. The captain ordered the Natives to stack their arms. It was a very tense moment. Emily calmly gathered her children around her and moved out of sight of the Natives who sat in the dirt in two rows on either side of the dishes. Meanwhile most of the men like Jacob and Mr. Elliott were concerned about their vulnerability in the event of a sudden act of treachery and so kept a firm grasp on their own weapons.

With a sudden start nearly all of the Native warriors leaped to their feet at once, let out a blood curdling yell and ran to their spears and retrieved them. They yelled and hollered and brandished their spears, terrifying the emigrants. Then in another odd but frightening twist they suddenly stabbed the tin plates with their spears on which the emigrants had so recently served them dinner.

The emigrant men who were not already armed retrieved their weapons and rejoined those who were. As one they leveled their firearms at the Native Americans. Their raucous display immediately came to a halt and all were still. Everyone on both sides appeared displeased. The leaders on both sides spoke in hushed tones with one another. Finally, the Native Americans turned away to their horses, mounted, and rode out of sight.

The destruction of so many plates made the emigrants very angry. Although, today it may not seem like much, there was no way to replace broken and ruined items along the way and with such limited space on such a journey as this they carried everything they needed and needed everything they carried. However, they were prudent enough to recognize that they were entirely at the mercy of the more numerous indigenous peoples and retaliation would likely backfire.

One or two days later several men called out in alarm when they spotted a small group of Native Americans once again riding toward the camp. The emigrants soon recognized them as the same band that had so recently visited them. This time however there were only a few men and instead of arms they carried "kettles, pans, plates, and cups."[35] The erstwhile warriors laid their burden in a pile inside the wagon camp and indicated that it was a gift to replace what they had destroyed. At first it was smiles all around as the Native American men watched each emigrant happily take from the pile what they had lost. However, after all of the emigrant families had satisfied each of their individual losses there were still several unclaimed items lying in the pile. The Native American leaders watching over this process quickly took offense at this slight, for in their eyes, their gift had been refused. The emigrants immediately became suspicious when they saw offended Natives scowl and utter guttural expressions of

---

[35] D'Arcy, "Reminiscences."

their disapproval. Undoubtedly, the indigenous men made the same observation concerning the emigrants. Leaders from both sides recognized where this was going and desperately tried to explain to each other that there was no bad intent. Finally, the leaders' exhortations to their followers to amity calmed their fears and the Native Americans left the emigrant camp peaceably and reconciled.

After this last confrontation with Native American warriors Emily and Jacob became concerned about the future of their family. Combined with long hot days, limited supplies, and the accidents they had just experienced at river crossings, they feared that their children might be orphaned, fore they knew they had traveled only a third of the distance and that the most difficult terrain yet still lay ahead. Committed to the journey and far from safety in any direction there was nothing they could do to make their lives more secure, but they could at least preserve their heritage. So Emily and Jacob took to examining their children on their family history. First, they taught them where they were from and whose family they were. Then they were questioned repeatedly and were expected to know: "What is your name? What is your father's name? Your mother's name? Where were you born? What State? What Country? Near what town? and about [their] grandparents...." [36] At times this catechism would take place formally in group as they stood in a row. At other times

---

[36] Ibid.

Emily questioned them as they sat with her in the wagon or as they worked side-by-side at their chores. Because formal education was unavailable on this extended journey, Emily applied this impromptu recitation to more traditional subjects like spelling and geography as well.

Over the next few weeks more bands of indigenous people shadowed the wagon train's movements across their lands. However, with no direct confrontation the emigrants became complacent. With all the stress and late-night chores, washing clothes and cleaning up after dinner, Emily was exhausted. She convinced Jacob to drive the horse-drawn wagon while she attempted to nap in the back.

As usual, the horse wagon was in the van of the train and all the children walked together near the center. Thus, there were no other emigrants nearby. Emily awoke with a start when she felt a hand clasp about her ankle. She looked up to see a very tall and powerfully built Native warrior, the largest she had ever seen, trying to pull her out of the back of the wagon. She instinctively pulled back and freed herself from his grasp. Undeterred, the Native raider reached in again and grabbed for her.

Emily could have called out to Jacob, but she was afraid that Jacob would kill the man and the other members of his band would cause trouble for the entire train. Emily quickly snatched her husband's gun and aimed it at the Native American man trying to kidnap her. He saw her self-confidence and tenacity, not to mention the gun she aimed at him. With a grunt the tall warrior gave up on his attempt to kidnap Emily and turned his horse and rode away.

The train slogged on mile after mile. They passed Independence Rock and stopped in the safety of Fort Hall in present day Idaho. Even there, safely ensconced within the protective walls they were not completely safe from the dangers and stresses of life on the trail. Little Jake fell deathly sick. Emily feared it was cholera. She sought the help of a doctor named McBride. Fortunately, however, it did not prove to be too serious and her "Little Red Bird" soon recovered.

After a short rest in Fort Hall the emigrants resumed their trek and unsurprisingly encountered more indigenous people. Frequently, the Native Americans entered the emigrants' camp, usually to barter. Whenever they did, they took a strong interest in little Jake because he had silvery blonde hair. Invariably the Native Americans would offer to trade something for him, typically horses. Their persistence in their effort to acquire him grated on the nerves of his parents.

This came to a head when a small band of indigenous people rode into camp and laid eyes on Jake, and called him "Tenas Ole Man," little old man.[37] Still on horseback they surrounded Jacob and demanded a trade. The wife of the "chief" offered to trade horses for "Tenas Ole Man," Jacob sternly refused and tried to disengage from them.

---

[37] Ibid. Marianne does not state what language or tribe this purports to be. In any event, on its face it looks like pidgin English.

Undeterred, the chief's wife kept bartering for little Jake. Finally, Jacob snapped and sarcastically said, "Yes, yes, alright." The Native American woman held out her arms so that the little boy could be lifted to her, and she laughed in triumphant satisfaction. However, Jacob thought she understood his response had all been made in jest, and he lifted his son up and held him on the horse in front of her.

Without warning, the chief's wife raised her rawhide quirt and violently struck Jacob on the hand with which he held Little Jake. Instinctively he pulled his hand back in pain releasing his grasp on his son.

Instantly the other Native American women closed ranks about their leader. But Jacob was faster. He lunged for the bridle of the chief's wife's horse. He missed, but his hand found Little Red Bird's leg instead. As the woman's horse leaped forward, she lost hold of the little boy and he fell headfirst but still in his father's grasp. Emily screamed, alerting other emigrants who were ever wary when indigenous people were in their camp. Quickly the two groups gathered into two angry circles, snarling and yelling at one another. Then, likely taking stock of their vulnerable position, the Native Americans laughed and tried to pass the episode off as one big joke. Finally, the band melted away and the emigrants went back to their chores. Jacob was left with a painful reminder on his hand in the form of a whip cut of how far from a joke this whole episode had been.

The children continued to make most of the journey walking alongside the wagons and only riding periodically to rest. For fun, the children mounted Cap and Dolly, riding the poor draft horses as they trudged along pulling the wagon. Sometimes the children climbed aboard the wagon only to jump off whenever they saw fit, regardless whether the wagon was moving or not. To get on, the children would watch the wagon and time their approach, darting in front of the front wheel hopping onto the broad portion of the tongue and pulling themselves up and in. To get out they climbed down to the same portion of the tongue and then jumped clear of the wheel.

Finally, the wagon train reached the longed-for Oregon Territory. In the Blue Mountains the children spied some big blue huckleberries lining the side of the road from their perch in the wagon. Josephine and Horton climbed down and leaped clear of the wagon in their usual manner. They turned on the huckleberry bushes, breaking whole branches off and then handing them up to Marianne, Ariminta, and Jake.

Marianne was not completely satisfied with this process, being dependent on her older siblings. Desiring to become more directly involved, she climbed down onto the tongue to jump off. There was a hole in the fat part of the tongue where many emigrants placed a hammer by sliding the handle through the hole allowing it to hang by the head. Unfortunately for Marianne, her long dress caught on the hammer head and instead of jumping cleanly away she slipped and fell right at the horses' heels. Before

Emily could do anything to stop the wagon, the front wheels rolled over her back and as she tried to crawl away the back wheels ran over her legs.

Emily was by then able to stop the wagon. She leaped down and swept Marianne up in her arms screaming and crying over her daughter. Marianne struggled to break free of her mother's grasp to go pick berries. Emily was quickly joined by other men and women who were in wagons behind hers. They stripped Marianne right there by the side of the road to see if she had been hurt. Only then did Marianne become alarmed, crying bitterly at the humiliation of this public body search. In the end no bruise or wound was found except to her pride.

Jacob and Emily split from the company at their earliest opportunity, and the family with their two wagons turned south. Marianne claimed that their family was among the first settlers to use the new Barlow Road. At Laurel Hill Jacob had to tie ropes to the wagons and, using trees for leverage, belay the wagons to the bottom with the help of Horton and Emily.

This was not a typical arid western Rocky Mountain forest. The forests along the Columbia River, the Willamette Valley and the areas appurtenant thereto were as they are today, lush and thickly vegetated. Not only was there a thick canopy overhead, but the forest floor was a dense tangle of undergrowth. Only sparsely populated by humans, whenever the Hunsaker clan stopped a stunning silence surely washed over them. Negotiating their way through this dark silent sea of green must have been exhausting and eerie work.

Life in Oregon

Jacob staked a claim on the Molalla River, but it was too late in the year for the family to build their own cabin, so the family joined another family, the Gordons, in a double log cabin— a two-room cabin where each family lived in one room. Today the idea of stuffing a seven-person family into a one-room cabin to live is unimaginable. However, in those days anything more than one room was a luxury and Marianne claimed that they were quite comfortable. By then Emily was quite far along on her sixth pregnancy and it was not too long after their arrival that Emily went into labor again.

Grandma Stewart had preceded the Hunsakers to Oregon. Jacob had already discovered where she lived, so when in the middle of the night Emily went into labor he leaped on Cap and rode several miles to Grandma Stewart's home. She had no horse or buggy of her own, so she retrieved a horse blanket and placed it on Cap's back just behind the saddle. "We must hurry, Jake," she told him and then climbed astride old Cap.[38] Jacob nudged Cap with his heel and away they loped back to the Hunsaker homestead. That night Emily gave birth to her fourth daughter, Sarah.

---

[38] Ibid.

All winter Emily and Mrs. Gordon made soap. In the Spring they placed their surplus soap into baskets. Emily saddled Cap and hung her basket from the saddle-horn and the ladies rode into Oregon City where they sold their soap. They used their profit to buy one hen for each of them and together they split the cost of one rooster. They brought their fowl prizes home and when their hens laid eggs, they watched them like hawks. Immediately after they hatched, they removed the chicks from the hen's nest. By the end of the year Emily had raised 102 chickens, and Mrs. Gordon nearly 100. They then sold their chickens to buy material to make dresses. Unfortunately, their cow later ate part of a dress Emily had made from her chicken profits as it hung out on a bush to dry after washing.

Since they had shelter, the following Spring Jacob and the family worked on the next priority, getting a crop in. After that, the men in the community worked together to erect a schoolhouse. It was a basic log structure of simple design—no windows, a puncheon floor and a "stick and mud fireplace and chimney."[39] The men made rough hewn benches and bored holes, into which they stuck pegs for legs. There were neither desks nor tables.

The children were eager to go back to school and when the schoolhouse was completed the idea of returning to school suddenly had a tangible reality to it. However, the community still needed to hire a teacher. Then one day Jacob returned home and

---

[39] Ibid. A puncheon floor is made of heavy timber slabs only roughly hewn.

announced with excitement that the town had just hired a teacher named Snyder and said to Emily "I must go to Oregon City tomorrow and get the children some books and leather to make shoes."[40]

The next day the children were positively giddy as they helped with chores, anticipating their father's return with books and shoes. Every few moments they glanced out to the road to see if he was coming. Like a watched pot, it seemed to take forever, and as it grew dark, he still had not returned. Every few minutes one of the children would wander to the door to listen in the dark for Jacob, but all they heard was the lonesome call of wolves.

Finally, they all froze when they heard Jacob's voice call to Horton, "Come and get these parcels while I put the horse to bed."[41] The children were beside themselves in anticipation of their new books. But when Emily "reverently" unrolled what appeared to them as nothing more than "printed newspapers," they were sorely disappointed. The children didn't know that there weren't textbooks on shelves waiting to be picked up. They did not realize that he too spent the day impatiently waiting for the books to come off the press and the books still had to be assembled.

After she fed Jacob, Emily went straight to work cutting, folding and gluing the children's books. Meanwhile, Jacob measured the children's feet so that he could make their shoes.

---

[40] Ibid.
[41] Ibid.

Once their feet were measured the children went to bed while their parents continued to work by the light of the fire and a candle. In the morning the children awoke to the sound of Emily working to get breakfast ready, while Jacob, having never slept, was still at work on the shoes. First, one child then another and another noticed sitting on the table sat their lovely new books. Now bound, the books were covered with material from Emily's prettiest calico dress, too worn to wear any longer. Glued to each was a piece of colored paper (an extravagance for those on the frontier) folded into a fan shape called a thumb-paper. The reader rested the cover's thumb-paper on their thumb as they read to reduce wear on the book itself.

Even after working all night Jacob had only completed one pair of shoes, Horton's. The ground had received a light dusting of snow during the night. Nevertheless, the girls were too excited by the prospect of the first day of school with new books in hand to be deterred from attending school. Horton dragged one foot to clear a path and the girls followed barefoot.

Before the day was out Jacob appeared at the schoolhouse with three more pairs of shoes draped over his shoulders by the laces which had been tied together. Class came to a halt as Josephine, Marianne and Ariminta put on their new shoes in front of the fire as all the other children looked on.

The children's delight with school was fairly short-lived, however. By this time emigrants were arriving in California and Oregon in large numbers. Jacob recognized the economic opportunity presented by the arrival of these emigrants reaching the west coast building homes, churches, schoolhouses and businesses. He knew lumber was now in demand and so he built a sawmill on Mill Creek at its confluence with the Columbia River in the shadow of Mount Saint Helens. In 1847 the family moved to the Saint Helens mill and established a new home. Near their new home Marianne and Ariminta found a large maple tree in whose ample shade they would often play. As they played games of make-believe, Ariminta and Marianne found beads hidden in the grass and half-buried in the dirt. Marianne and Ariminta took to calling the tree the "Indian Tree" because of the treasure they found at its base.

At the mill Jacob built a deck over the bank and some of the shallows. Emily often stored butter in the cool shallows in the shade of the deck. Jacob built a large sturdy paddlewheel that extended into the stream's current, and thus powered the wheel. A drive shaft connected the paddlewheel to a saw blade. Jacob rolled logs onto a cradle and then slowly drew the cradle with the new log loaded on it into the turning saw blade cutting them into planks which he then removed and stacked opposite the new logs. Emily often assisted Jacob in rolling the large logs into the cradle using pry bars and a great deal of physical effort. Sometimes however, Emily would sit on the stack of sawed lumber sewing as Jacob rolled the heavy logs into position. One day as Emily sat, focused on her sewing, Jacob strained, prying the log up into position when it suddenly rolled up and over the lip and onto the carriage.

However, with its tremendous weight it rolled up and over the opposite lip and onto the deck beyond. Jacob yelled and the log pounded the deck startling Emily. She immediately dropped her needle and thread and leaped to her feet, but before she could move the log slammed into her, pinning her foot against the stack of rough lumber.

Jacob ran over and frantically pried the log as Emily screamed in agony. Her young daughters came running just as Jacob rolled the log off Emily's foot. Jacob helped her to sit. Once her boot was loosened from her foot it instantly swelled. Not long after, it turned an ugly black and blue.

Jacob worried that Emily's foot might have to be amputated. When he expressed his concern to Emily she cried, "Never! I'll die first!"[42] She applied her own remedies and hobbled around on a cane for a long time. She hired some local Native women, but she felt they needed active supervision which she was not able to do. Consequently, Josephine, though only seven or eight years of age, had to assume much of the duties around the house that Emily had done before.

Sisters of Notre Dame

As Emily convalesced, she and Jacob spent many hours talking about their future plans. Foremost of Emily's concerns was that the children needed an education and that they lived in near isolation at the St. Helens mill.

---

[42] Ibid.

Emily finally convinced Jacob to sell the St. Helens mill for the sake of the children. So, in the fall of 1848 the family loaded their few belongings on a flat bottom boat and sailed and rowed past a new settlement called Portland to a point just below Oregon City where they settled—for the moment.

Near Oregon City the Sisters of Notre Dame had established a school for girls. Jacob and Emily enrolled Josephine, Marianne, and Ariminta as day students. However, just as the discovery of gold at Sutter's mill drove Henry Burmester to move to San Francisco to sell hardware, that same gold rush created an extraordinary and lucrative demand for lumber in California and Jacob wanted to build a new mill on the Washougal River to exploit it. Emily and Jacob then enrolled the three oldest girls as boarding students instead of just day students. They left Horton in the care of Miss Mary Johnson who also ran a school that he attended, leaving Jacob and Emily with only their two youngest children, Jake and Sarah, to care for. Thus, they were able to seek their fortune with another lumber mill, this time on the Washougal.

Back with the Sisters of Notre Dame, Josephine, Marianne, and Ariminta were homesick from the moment their parents said goodbye. Not long after their parents left, another student, a little older than Josephine, reinforced the children's worst fear when she explained that most of the girls at Notre Dame were orphans which she said were children whose parents had died or abandoned them for the gold fields.

Nevertheless, the girls carried on, getting used to the school routine and making new friends. Late one evening Marianne went to the outhouse with several other young girls her age. Unbeknownst to them, one of the older girls crept up to the outhouse and began to pound on the door and call to them in a loud and gruff voice. Terrified, the young girls screamed, afraid they were being accosted by a drunken old man. One of the Sisters heard the screaming and fearing the worst, ran straight for the outhouse. However, once she determined what had really happened, she punished the younger girls by making them take their next few meals while kneeling at the table instead of seated in a chair. Marianne insisted, until the end of her days, that the real culprit, the prankster who had pounded on the outhouse door and growled, was never punished because she was the granddaughter of the primary patron of the school.

While the children lived and studied in Oregon City, Emily and Jacob began their operation on the Washougal. By October the leaves turned "red and gold, mingled with the dark green of firs, cedars, and hemlock," during a beautiful but extraordinarily dry Indian summer.

The lovely autumn weather was compromised when the forest in the vicinity of the Washougal mill was set ablaze. The fire was the most severe that anyone could recall. When it threatened the mill, Jacob and his employees worked feverishly to save the enterprise. They were joined by local Native Americans and soon all were so covered by soot, dirt and burns that they were indistinguishable, one from the other.

Jacob begged Emily to flee to a place of safety. From the fire line he sent men to get her to leave but she steadfastly refused. He even came off the line himself at one point and physically removed her, but she came right back.

The fire continued to close in on the mill and the men bravely battled on against the blaze directly. Alarmed that the fire now threatened the mill, Emily went inside and located the barrel of blasting powder that they stored there. She turned the barrel onto its side and rolled it into the river, for fear that it might explode and injure the men. Only then did she withdraw to a safer location. In the end the men and Emily saved the mill, but all of the cabins were lost to the fire. So, as October turned into November, Jacob and Emily were forced to return to the home on the Clackamas River that Emily had chosen before they left for the Washougal.

Soon after arriving in the new house, before they could even retrieve their older children from the boarding schools, Emily again went into labor. Jacob immediately took off on his horse to bring back none other than Grandma Stewart. Emily gave birth to a boy they named Lycurgus on November 4, 1849.

After the birth of Lycurgus, Jacob and Emily sent word to the Sisters to bring the girls to their new home. Somehow the word leaked out and one of their classmates told Marianne her parents were back and that she now had a baby brother before the Sisters could tell her. The camp on the Washougal was remote with no rail, boat or even mail connection to Oregon City. Consequently, the girls had not heard a word from their parents since they had arrived at Notre Dame. By this time Marianne was convinced she was an "orphan" turned over to the Sisters for good, so she did not believe the girl. But sure enough, Sister Mary Berni came to Josephine, Marianne, and Ariminta and told them to gather their belongings, for they were going home to see their mother.

As the beautiful "Indian summer" gave way to the frosty chill of November, the girls packed for their journey with Sister Mary Berni to Clackamas.

To these three young girls full of anticipation the trip must have seemed to take an eternity. "What a long way we had to go over the lowland filled with brush, and up a little rise, into the log cabin of one room."[43] There, they rushed inside where they found their mother lying in bed. She eagerly greeted them with outstretched arms. But just as soon as they saw their mother, the three girls noticed that piled on a blanket in a basket by the bed lay ripe juicy tomatoes and peaches. The Sisters had maintained the girls on a restricted diet so after the difficult walk through the brush the girls were famished and ravenously attacked the fruit despite Sister Mary's admonishments. However, Sister Mary proved herself a prophetess when Josephine, Marianne and Ariminta were sick all night long.

---

[43] D'Arcy, "Reminiscences."

The Clackamas River Bridge War

When Jacob and Emily moved into their Clackamas River home there were only two ways to cross the river, both were ferry sites, one owned by Mr. Cason and another owned by Joseph Henderson. Soon after their arrival Mr. Cason secured a monopoly on the river crossing traffic when he purchased Henderson's ferry as well. To reach Cason's ferry the traveler took the main road past Cason's home and farm to the river and then turned parallel to the river traveling downstream to the crossing site, skirting Cason's farm fields.

Early in 1852 Jacob had another entrepreneurial idea: build a toll bridge across the Clackamas River right where the main road met the river. He shared his idea with a few trusted friends who told him that they thought the idea was sound and encouraged him to proceed.

Mr. Cason soon learned of Jacob's plan for the toll bridge. Because the bridge would compete with his ferries, he was not keen on the idea. Accordingly, he quietly went around to as many people in the county as he could reach and got them to sign a petition authorizing him to change the course of the road so that it crossed his field directly to his ferry landing and then to Oregon City. This would cut off direct access to the bridge.

When Jacob belatedly learned of Cason's petition, he went out seeking signatures on his own protest of the petition. Some people signed both while others, once committed, refused to switch though their feelings might have been favoring the bridge.

The dispute became heated and divided the community. However, the parties reached a temporary compromise which allowed for a road to cross Cason's field but also provided for roads on both sides of the river from bridge site to ferry landings.

That was the first battle in the Clackamas River Bridge war. It ended in a draw, but the war was far from over. The right to build the bridge was submitted to the legislature where it became a controversial political issue hotly debated between Democrats and Whigs. When the bill came up for a vote it passed. However, according to the legislation Jacob had to complete the project by a specified date.

Jacob began work in the spring, but the river was high and running hard, making the work difficult, but also preventing Mr. Cason from operating his ferry. Jacob pushed ahead with his work despite the difficulties.

Finally, Jacob completed all of the spans except the last one. It was late and getting dark. Jacob left the timbers necessary for the final span tied to the bank ready for assembly the next day. However, in the morning when he arrived at the bridge to complete the project, he discovered that someone had cut the ropes that had held the timbers together and the wood had floated away downstream.

There was never any direct evidence of who had cut the wood free but circumstantial facts pointed to Mr. Cason. In addition to motive, Cason had been in Salem all day but arrived in

Oregon City at night and had walked home using the nearly completed bridge to cross the rushing river.

Jacob was devastated—his time limit set by the legislature was fast approaching. Nevertheless, he did not give up. He went out and recruited help with wood cutting. Because the time was so near, he had the men prepare only rough temporary planks. With the extra help Jacob soon had the bridge construction back on schedule. When Jacob arrived in the morning to make the finishing touches on the bridge, he found Cason had earlier sent his two sons, Add and Joe, to demolish the bridge. The two boys had drilled holes into large rocks (presumably abutting the wood bridge structure). The boys had then filled the holes with gun powder, which they detonated much to Jacob's astonishment.

The first blast only caused superficial damage, so the boys started pounding the drill into another rock. Jacob ordered the boys to stop and leave the bridge alone, but they refused to listen. Once they had a hole of sufficient depth, they poured gun powder into it. Jacob scooped up water from the river and doused the powder charge before the boys could detonate it. The Cason boys and Jacob kept up this strange game of drilling, loading and dousing until Add and Joe finally gave up and left.

Jacob ran home yelling that he was going to get his gun and protect his property. Emily heard his ranting and finally got him calm enough to explain what had happened. When he tried to leave with his rifle, she grabbed hold of it and would not let go. She demanded he talk to his lawyer "Judge Waite."[44]

Jacob finally relented and went to see Judge Waite who obtained an injunction barring any further interference from the Casons, and Jacob was able to complete the bridge.

In the fall of 1852, around the same time that Jacob initiated his counter-petition seeking public support for his Clackamas River Bridge a family of emigrants from the east arrived, two sisters with their husbands and children. Several of them were very sick with typhus. It was getting cold and they had no place to stay.

The Hunsakers took the ill family members into their home while the rest of the emigrant clan took up residence in an abandoned shelter they found nearby. Soon after taking them in, Marianne came down with the illness followed by the baby, Katie. During that winter and spring all of the children came down with the disease; Horton and then Josephine died from it. Emily continued to help the emigrants throughout and so it was inevitable that she too fell ill, delirious and burning with fever, before summer began. Eventually, Emily recovered. But throughout she worked so unceasingly that when she suffered a "slight stroke of paralysis" after her next child, the family blamed it on overexertion. Ironically, only Jacob who had been

---

[44] During the nineteenth century in the Pacific Northwest at least, the title "Judge" appears to be attributed to all members of the bar and not just members of the bench. Thomas R. Donaldson, *Idaho of Yesterday*, (Westport: Greenwood Press, 1970), 203.

chronically ill in Illinois, never suffered from typhus that year. Perhaps he had been too busy selling the bridge idea and then constructing it to be exposed.

After Jacob completed the bridge, he built a gate and then employed Marianne, Jake, and Curg (Lycurgus) to man the gate and collect the tolls. At one point a rambunctious group of indigenous people from the local Klamath tribe decided to race their horses on the bridge. But before they could do so Jake shut the gate. At the time the Klamath were, understandably, very bitter toward the white settlers for despoiling their traditional hunting grounds. However, the other local tribes, Clackamas and Molalla, got on very well with whites in general and Jacob in particular. Jacob often hired them and made small loans to them when they were in need.

One of the racing Klamath men yelled down from his horse at Jake, ordering him to open the gate. When Jake refused, the man pulled out a knife and dismounted.

Marianne said, "Jake, he will kill us if we don't open up."

Jake replied, "He will kill us anyway, so I will not open up the gate."

Marianne began to chant, "Oh God please save us!" Moments later she saw not God but her father purposefully striding toward them, axe in hand.

When Jacob reached the bridge, he dropped the axe and grabbed the first menacing Klamath man by the waist and quickly hurled him off the bridge into the river. Before either Native or child could think, Jacob grabbed the second Klamath and flung him after the first. At which point the remaining Klamaths scattered.

Several Clackamas and Molalla who had been watching the confrontation cheered and called Jacob a good friend.[45] But the bridge had been plagued by strife and controversy since its inception and this was the final straw. Jacob sold the bridge to Mr. Cason and bought an apple orchard and moved his family once again.

<u>Ariminta and Theodore</u>

After the deaths of the oldest children, Ariminta and Marianne assumed more responsible roles within the family. Marianne became the caretaker for the young children each morning and Ariminta prepared breakfast for the family; they were only 11 and 10 years of age respectively. During this same time Emily gave birth to her ninth child, she would eventually give birth to twelve children before her death at age 54.

As Ariminta and Marianne became teens they were visited by boys including Joe and Add Cason. The Hunsaker girls and Cason boys were able to set aside their differences and became close friends, but the girls never let the boys live down their role in the bridge war. The boys took the teasing in stride however and both Ariminta and Marianne recognized that the bridge had

---

[45] Marianne claimed they said, "Hias skookum Hunsaker, hias close Tillicum, hias tyee Hunsaker." She asserts in her memoir that the expression translates to Jacob was a good friend.

severely undercut Mr. Cason's business. They understood that it was only the stress of economic survival, and nothing personal that drove Mr. Cason to press the boys into service as guerillas.

Ariminta was very adept in school and by the age of 17 taught the primary age children at the local school. Marianne thought Ariminta was their father's favorite and therefore he seemed quite protective of her. In any case, he was intensely proud of her.

Ariminta was not only intelligent but also headstrong and a romantic. She took up a correspondence with several young suitors, including "Harvey Scott, later editor of the Oregonian; W. Lair Hill, afterward one of the foremost lawyers and judges on the coast."[46] At the same time a friend of hers told a young man named Theodore Burmester about "Minnie" as she was by then known. Intrigued, he wrote to her and Minnie began a regular correspondence with him as well. Often Minnie included references to the other men to whom she was also corresponding and at times would even enclose the letter of one man to her in the letter to another!

Theodore was quickly enamored by Minnie though he had never actually seen her. Finally, he could no longer hold back his desire to meet her and so without warning, much less invitation, he rode from Salem to meet her. He arrived and asked Jacob for a job. Though not an unheard-of request, he seemed different from

---

[46] D'Arcy, "Reminiscences."

the usual type that sought such employment. Marianne thought him "sociable and agreeable" though at the same time "occasionally a little saucy and impertinent."[47]

Minnie had not yet returned from school when Theodore revealed who he really was and why he had come. He asked all those present not to tell Minnie when she arrived. But little nine-year-old Kate, secretly outed him to her. Minnie danced around the room chanting, "Now we will have some fun!"

Minnie joined the family but hid from everyone that she knew this man was her pen pal. The family sat politely attentive as Theodore tried to impress them with "one of his half witty, half saucy speeches."[48] When he finished she walked out of the room and into the parlor and began playing the piano. Theodore followed her into the parlor. Her countenance feigned a look of displeasure that he should follow.

Theodore ignored her expression and said simply, "Well Minnie, how do you do?"

"Very well Theodore, how are you?" she replied.[49]

Theodore extended his hand, she reciprocated, and the couple shook hands.

Broad smiles must have spread across the faces of each for it was love at first sight, or touch, as it were. Theodore and Minnie engaged in uninterrupted conversation until the rest of the family

---

[47] Ibid.
[48] Ibid.
[49] Ibid.

began to go to bed. Neither Theodore nor Minnie wanted the night to end but Minnie's father felt differently. Since everyone else was going to bed he would not allow Theodore to remain in their house alone with Minnie unchaperoned. Accordingly, Jacob ordered the young couple to break off their conversation for the night.

Theodore did not like Jacob's order and argued with him, "I have come all the way from Salem to see Minnie and I cannot really get to know her with all the family gathered around." Jacob was unmoved and remained insistent that the couple call it a night. Although they continued to talk for a short time after everyone left, Theodore finally bid Minnie adieu for the evening.

After he left, Theodore began to dwell on the notion that he should be allowed to spend time alone with Minnie. That night Theodore decided he would demand to spend the next day in Minnie's exclusive company. Meanwhile her father came to understand the "seriousness of Theodore's intentions" and in his mind drew a line in the sand. "Had [Theodore] been President of the United States, Father would not have thought him good enough for his 'Mimi,'" Marianne later wrote.

Bright and early the next morning, Theodore presented his demand to Jacob and his family. This time however, Minnie too rebelled and sided with Theodore and refused to attend her class. She even recruited Marianne to serve as substitute teacher for her.

Jacob objected and in the midst of his loud protestations, Theodore and Minnie fled the house. They spent the entire day walking around and through the orchard thoroughly engrossed in conversation. When they finally returned to the house at dinner time, Jacob expressed his displeasure which precipitated an angry response from Theodore, the Hunsaker's first introduction to what they soon learned was a prominent characteristic of the young gentleman. Minnie finally intervened. She pulled Theodore aside. She urged him to leave for now, but she "gave him her word" that she was nearly of age and that when she turned eighteen, he could return, and she would be his.

Theodore, sufficiently calmed, finally acquiesced and left the Hunsaker house, but refused to leave town. For several days he prowled around town trying to find ways to meet up with Minnie. For her part, Minnie sent messages expressing her undying love for him through Marianne.

Jacob steadfastly opposed Theodore. As if this were some mere child's obsession, Jacob thought that if he could distract Minnie she would simply forget about Theodore. So, he abruptly decided to take his family to San Francisco, a long and expensive journey in that day.

The family stayed in San Francisco for a month. During that time arrangements were made for Minnie to take charge of a "young ladies' seminary in Healdsburg, California."[50] However, in April, soon after she returned, she resumed exchanging letters with Theodore, this time surreptitiously through one of her old

---

[50] Ibid.

schoolmates. For this intrigue she did not even trust her beloved sister, Marianne.

Near the end of April, Minnie spent a week getting her clothes in order, cleaning her white dress and other summer dresses. Marianne asked why she was getting her summer dresses ready so early. Minnie just answered that she just wanted them ready before she left home for the young ladies' seminary.

On April 28, 1861, her birthday, Minnie spent the day with Marianne visiting neighbors. Minnie wore a new dress. That evening Emily did not feel well, and she asked Minnie to take the baby, Winnie, for the night. Minnie took the baby straight to Marianne and asked *her* to watch the baby for the night. Marianne worshipped her sister, and readily agreed. Minnie handed over their baby sister and said, "Good night Mary."[51] Minnie turned and left the room. She walked down the stairs to get a pitcher of water. She saw her father standing alone on the back porch. She stepped out the door, hugged her father and kissed him, and then said, "Good night Father," before going back up to bed.

For a time, Minnie lay in bed, likely, her eyes wide open, her heart pounding with anticipation, wearing her white dress she so recently cleaned and pressed. In the middle of the night she heard horses ride up just outside. The excitement and tension at this most dangerous moment must have been terrific. She grabbed her bag filled with all her dresses and placed a carefully worded

---

[51] Ibid.

note she had written on top of her bureau. Quietly she carried her bag down the stairs and out the door.

Outside she found Theodore with two horses as she expected, but another figure also with a horse stood close by. As she closed in on the two men in the dark, she recognized the other man as the Justice of the Peace.

Theodore whispered, "This will be a fine joke on your father when he discovers that we were married on his own porch."

Minnie demurred, "I want to be able to see the man who marries us."

Theodore relented and the three of them rode off in the dark for the "rooms of a schoolmate" where they were married.

The next morning Jacob called out from the foot of the stairs, "Minnie, it's time to to wake up and begin the day." Minnie was always quick to respond to her father's call in the morning, but this time only silence greeted his call.

Jacob immediately suspected something was wrong. He raced up the stairs and into her room. On the bureau he found the note addressed to him in her precise teacher's handwriting. Minnie explained to her father that she had left to marry Theodore, begging him to forgive them.

Jacob burst into forlorn cries, "Oh, she's gone, she's gone! Oh Minnie, Minnie!"

After they were wed, Theodore and Ariminta rode on horseback to Aurora and caught a stagecoach to Salem where they lived for the next few months.

Chapter 3: Lucretia, "I Love You Darling"

Several months after they were wed, Theodore and Ariminta moved from Salem to LeGrand, Oregon. The discovery of silver ignited a rush of fortune seekers, this time from the west coast into the second range of mountains to the east. There, Theodore ran a hotel. Ariminta became pregnant. Her first two children did not survive beyond birth. However, her third child born the day before her birthday on April 27, 1865, did live. The young parents named him Frank. Later that same year, Theodore and his little family moved to Ada County, Idaho Territory where Theodore filed a homestead claim in November.

On the homestead claim six miles south of Fort Boise, Theodore built a house and operated a small ranch and farm with a couple of hired hands. Meanwhile he took up the practice of law which was his real source of income. Ariminta took care of the home and in 1868, gave birth to her fourth child, another son, William.

During the second half of the 1860's the legal community in Boise consisted of a little more than a dozen active attorneys.[52] The practice of law was a general practice, not the highly specialized practice that it is today. Theodore and his partner handled various criminal and civil cases, but primarily the firm filed liens to perfect judgments on debt they obtained at discount. A contemporary described the partners, Scaniker and Burmester as

---

[52] Donaldson, *Idaho of Yesterday*, 203.

being known "for charging large fees and for seldom, if ever, losing or lowering fees. Scaniker had the dignity of the firm, and Burmester had the push!"[53]

The territorial governor of Idaho during the second half of the decade was David W. Ballard. Ballard was short with a slightly rounded physique. He had blue eyes with sandy hair and beard. He was a physician by training and had come west from Indiana in 1855 by wagon train. He was an affable gentleman, agreeable, with a self-effacing sense of humor. A radical Republican, he had been appointed in 1866, post Civil War, but was surrounded by secession sympathizing Democrats.[54] Consequently, during the early years of his administration he expended copious amounts of political capital fighting off Democrats' "tempest in a tea pot" political attacks against him. Governor Ballard refused to allow the legislature to be paid, pursuant to Federal law, until the secessionists Democrats swore an oath against Confederacy, to which they took exception.[55] The territory's lone delegate to the U.S. House of Representatives, E. D. Holbrook used petitions and fraudulent accusations encouraging President Johnson to suspend Ballard. The President temporarily suspended Ballard and even appointed another man as governor. However, the popular outcry was so great that the United States Senate refused to confirm the new appointment and

---

[53] Ibid, 207.
[54] Leonard J. Arrington, *History of Idaho,* vol. 1, (Moscow: University of Idaho Press, 1994), 288.
[55] Ibid.

Johnson finally backed off and Ballard finished his term.[56] During much of this time Ballard's pay was suspended and he subsisted on income generated by his medical practice.[57]

Ballard's strongest ally was James S. Reynolds, the editor and proprietor of the Idaho Tri-Weekly Statesman. Reynolds was a tall bearded man. His large gruff voice complemented his larger than life character.

James S. Reynolds. Image no. 208, Idaho State Archives.

---

[56] Donaldson, *Idaho of Yesterday*, 242-251; Arrington, *History of Idaho*, vol. 1, 290.
[57] Merle W. Wells, *Idaho: An Illustrated History*, (Boise: The Idaho State Historical Society, 1976), 44.

Idaho Tri-Weekly Statesman. Image no. 73-2-47, Idaho State Archives.

Reynolds originally hailed from New York but was living in Wisconsin when his first wife died.[58] He moved to the Dalles, Oregon and arrived with two men who were brothers, and coincidently named Reynolds, but who were no relation to James. The three men agreed to start a newspaper. After they rounded up investors and James located printing equipment in the Dalles, James was set up as the Editor of the Tri-Weekly Statesman.

Big, tough and opinionated, Reynolds proudly claimed that he never carried a firearm in a community where nearly everyone did. Neither he nor his newspaper shied away from zealously expressing his views in support of the Republican Party and opposing judges he did not like. One judge in particular he did

---

[58] Donaldson, *Idaho of Yesterday*, 125.

not like was David Noggle, and he spared no expense in time or treasure in his personal crusade to remove Noggle from the bench.

In a fight or a quarrel, James Reynolds was unflappable. From 1869 to 1872 the office of the Idaho Tri-Weekly Statesman was located in a "two-story frame building opposite the City Hotel, at Seventh and Idaho Streets."[59] Reynolds lived in the upper floor of the building and slept in the front room. This room opened onto a small porch held up by two slender columns. One night Reynolds lay awake on his bed in the dark with his windows open. Suddenly a man's head appeared in the window which he could see clearly in the moonlight. The man quietly climbed in through the window and then lit a lantern. Reynolds did not move at first but watched as the man began to rummage through a pile of papers and things on the floor. Although he could see that the intruder was armed with a short club, he did not become alarmed. Rather, he remained calm throughout, watching the man in calm silence until finally, "Jim sat up in bed and asked, 'Excuse me, pardy, but who are you?'"[60]

Surprised by Reynolds' sudden appearance the man replied, "'I'm a robber!'" "'Ain't you skeered?'"

"'Nope!' said Jim, stealthily reaching for his gun. 'On the contrary, I'm enjoying myself. But say, what are you hunting for in that pile?'"

"'Money!' said the thief, vigorously thrusting about."

---

[59] Ibid., 128.
[60] Ibid.

"'Money?' Queried Jim, as if puzzled. 'Think you'll find any? You do? Well, I'll get up and help you hunt. I've been here for six years without finding any.'"

At that point Reynolds pulled up the gun and leveled the muzzle on the burglar. Seeing that the gig was up, the burglar ran for the window as Reynolds yelled at him, "You get!" The man happily obliged him, leaped through the window and slid down one column and disappeared into the night.[61]

Reynolds' other passion was the Boise Vigilance Committee. Some of the town's leading citizens formed the committee in 1865 after observing the miraculous clean-up job the Payette Vigilance Committee did there.[62]

In the early 1860s robbers, gamblers, and Civil War refugees flocked to Idaho Territory along with the miners seeking their fortune. Ruffians quickly dominated and intimidated local communities, seizing local political offices and intimidating juries. In response, "citizens groups" formed in Lewiston, Idaho City, Payette and other Idaho towns. William J. McConnell led the Payette Vigilantes and coordinated its efforts with other committees from La Grande, Oregon to Montana. Payette was so successful in banishing and hanging outlaws that it converted a

---

[61] Ibid.
[62] Ibid., 165; Arrington, *History of Idaho*, vol. 1, 225.

wild west outlaw town into a bucolic community as safe and peaceful as any in the Union.[63]

David Updyke was the leader of a violent outlaw gang. However, he was able to assert significant influence in the Democratic party dominated legislature. Through that body he got himself appointed Ada County Sheriff. From that position he ruled through brutal repression and abuse of office.

In 1866 an Updyke man named John C. Clark murdered a nineteen-year-old boy named Ruben Raymond after the latter testified against the former. That same night Boise Vigilantes removed Clark from his jail cell and hanged him.

Updyke could read the writing on the wall and attempted to flee town with another gang ally named John Dixon. Nevertheless, around fifteen of the Boise men caught up with the two men approximately thirty miles from Boise when they were holed up in a cabin. The vigilantes took the two men inside a shed. There, they informed Updyke of his fate, to which he did not protest. The next day prospectors found Updyke's corpse hanging from a rafter in the shed with a note attached: "Dave Updyke, the aider [sic] of murderers and horse thieves. XXX."[64] About four miles from where Updyke met his demise, the vigilantes gave John Dixon a similar farewell. On this model began the Boise Vigilance Committee which secretly met and voted people's fate

---

[63] Donaldson, *Idaho of Yesterday.*, 172-74; Arrington, *History of Idaho*, vol. 1, 223-25.
[64] Donaldson, *Idaho of Yesterday*, 166.

and then meted out the punishment—death or banishment—they felt the transgression merited. On the positive side, crime apparently did decrease some have argued.[65]

Governor Ballard and James Reynolds were just two of the acquaintances within Ariminta's and Theodore's social circle. In addition, they were of course friendly with other members of the bar. There was Theodore's partner, S. P. Scaniker as well as the studious Henry Prickett and the eloquent Frank Ganahl. Theodore ran for exercise with a young southern expatriate named Romily E. Foote who carried the title of "Major."[66] In the 1870 census he claimed to be from Mississippi, though his name does not appear on any Confederate army rolls available today from any Mississippi unit. Russell B. Morford was a friendly but lazy lawyer who could not stay away from gambling—or debt.[67] His other problem was his wife, Amanda, who was admired for her physical beauty but was a notorious flirt.[68] These were people with whom Theodore worked and who came into their home when they entertained.

Ariminta and Theodore's ranch house was located approximately six miles below Boise on the River Road.[69] Theodore farmed part of his land and employed two men to do the

---

[65] Arrington, *History of Idaho*, vol. 1, 224-25.

[66] Most sources, including the 1870 census, spell Romily Foote with an "e" at the end although in a few places it is spelled "Foot."

[67] "The Burmester Trial!" *Idaho (Boise) Tri-Weekly Statesman*, Jan. 11, 1870.

[68] Donaldson, *Idaho of Yesterday*, 206.

[69] "Terrible Tragedy—Fiendish Attempt at Outrage—House Burned to Ashes, Etc.," *Idaho (Boise) Tri-Weekly Statesman*, May 18, 1869, 3.

work. These two men, Thomas Bevans and a German immigrant named John Konapeck lived in the upstairs rooms of the house.[70]

Ariminta had misgivings about John Konapeck.[71] She expressed her fears to Theodore and asked him to get rid of the ranch hand. But Konapeck was apparently a hard worker. Theodore didn't want to discharge this dependable servant and convinced himself that Ariminta's concerns were just based on exaggerated "female feelings" and not based on real evidence. So Theodore refused to let the man go.

By all accounts Ariminta was a doting mother to her two young boys. She ruled the house and was a gracious hostess to their many friends. She was also a devoted wife. With such a playful loving spirit one can imagine she and Theodore sitting side by side on the piano bench singing together while she played. She had many friends and likely entertained these friends at their house.

There were only a few judges in Idaho Territory during the 1860s with large tracts of "empty" land in their jurisdiction. As a result, the judges and attorneys traveled throughout the territory to the various towns to hear civil and criminal cases. Thus, Theodore's work required him to travel and routinely leave Ariminta and the boys alone on the ranch.

On Saturday morning, May 14, 1869, Theodore woke up very early, dressed and caught the stage for Payette at 4:00 a.m. It

---

[70] Ibid.; D'Arcy, "Reminiscences."
[71] D'Arcy, "Reminiscences."

was a thirty-mile journey in a coach with nothing like modern automobile suspension or even rubber tires over dirt roads likely deeply rutted. In Payette, Theodore attended to one of his cases.

Meanwhile, back home, the day likely began like most days for Ariminta and the boys. Thomas Bevans and John Konapeck went to the fields to work. Frank, the older boy, joined Thomas in the field. Ariminta remained in the house, presumably doing chores while caring for young William.

Early in the afternoon, Konapeck injured his finger and came into the house seeking help from Ariminta. He followed her into the bedroom to the bureau where she bent down to open the lowest drawer to get a clean rag to tend to the wound.

With Ariminta bent over and facing away from him, Konapeck suddenly grabbed her by the throat from behind with one hand and lifted her dress with the other. Ariminta fought her way free from his grasp, however, now enraged he assaulted her with savage fury. He threw her to the floor and beat her repeatedly with his fists and stomped on her.[72]

Konapeck left Ariminta in the bedroom for dead and went upstairs and retrieved baby William. He then carried the infant outside and laid him in the back of a wagon. When Konapeck went upstairs Ariminta crawled to the bedroom door and locked it.

---

[72] Two letters sent to Marianne, Ariminta's sister, describing the event survive, one from her father, Jacob, and another from Theodore. Jacob's letter which is double hearsay claims Konapeck beat her with a pistol. Theodore's letter does not mention beating with any instrument. The newspaper reported that he beat her with fists and stomped on her. "Terrible Tragedy," *Tri-Weekly Statesman*, May 18, 1869.

Konapeck heard her movement and returned with his revolver. He fired two shots through the door, both missed Ariminta. She attempted to defend herself, hurriedly retrieving a shot gun from her closet. When Konapeck appeared in the window she aimed and fired at him, but all she heard was a dull click as the gun misfired.

Konapeck took aim through the window and emptied his revolver, firing four more shots. One bullet struck Ariminta in the hip and she fell to the floor in agony. Eventually she heard Konapeck go back in the house and walk up the staircase, but not before he set the house on fire.

Thomas Bevans and little Frank out in the fields heard the gun shots and then saw the smoke billow up from the house. They knew something was grievously wrong and so came running back to the house. Konapeck, Theodore surmised, could see Thomas running toward the house and so he found Bevans' revolver and fired two times trying to kill himself.

Ariminta heard the shots and suspected what Konapeck had done to himself. She also smelled the smoke and knew he had set the house on fire. Her greatest agony, greater than the pain in her stomach, was the thought that her baby was still in the house. She did not know that Konapeck, who inexplicably adored William while detesting Frank, had already taken the boy outside. With thoughts of saving her baby from burning alive, she crawled directly to the source of the fire. She tried desperately to put the fire out, but the pain from her stomach wound kept her from being able to beat back the flames. The fire only grew and forced her to retreat and she clawed her way out of the inferno. By this time, she was not only in excruciating pain but she believed her infant child still lived but was helpless against the growing conflagration. She lay just outside the house screaming as Thomas Bevans and Frank came running up from the field panting.

Meanwhile, Konapeck had not quite managed to kill himself with the gun, and he soon realized he would be burned to death instead. So, with gunshot wounds he too began to crawl out of the smoke-filled upper room to a window or door ledge above the porch. From there he fell to the porch below. But in the end, he was not able to escape, and the fire caught up to him there where he died.[73]

Thomas Bevans carried Ariminta away from the house, which was by then fully engulfed, to a place of safety. Eventually someone, probably Bevans, discovered William where Konapeck had placed him—in the wagon.

Ariminta and the boys were taken to the house of a neighbor named John Bixby. They summoned her doctor, named Wagner. He came immediately and was soon joined by several other physicians, including Governor Ballard and Doctor Bailey who would subsequently write a letter to Jacob and Emily Hunsaker.

---

[73] "Terrible Tragedy," *Tri-Weekly Statesman*, May 18, 1869. Theodore's letter differs on this point claiming Konapeck died from two self inflicted gun shots.

Meanwhile a rider was sent posthaste to Payette to fetch Theodore. Upon receiving the news Theodore later wrote, "What a ride I had that night. Think of riding 17 miles in an hour and ¼ to find my wife murdered and my house in ashes—riding with the speed of race horses [*sic*] to the carnival of death—Oh that night's ride I can never forget...."

The single bullet entered at Ariminta's hip and passed into her abdomen. It pierced her bowel and that, in those days before the discovery of the germ was a sure death sentence. Though she was attended by a host of doctors they had no ability to open her up, clean her abdominal cavity of the spilt excrement from the torn bowel and close the bowel and the surgical opening all while replacing blood lost due to the surgery. Instead, they fed her beef tea and were pleased when she rested and were encouraged when she stopped vomiting.[74]

Soon after the shooting, all of Boise knew about the incident and the paper updated them on "Mrs. B's" condition. John Konapeck's charred corpse was left in place for two days, a ghastly specter for the living to gawk at, and toward which, they likely expressed their frustration at their inability to inflict more suffering and humiliation on this "fiend."

Ariminta clung to life suffering excruciating pain. When Theodore arrived after "the horse race to the carnival of death," Ariminta was still alive. Despite the pain, she was still lucid and

---

[74] "Hopes of Recovery," *Idaho (Boise) Tri-Weekly Statesman*, May 18, 1869, 2.

able to talk to her beloved. She told him what had happened. At some point though they both knew she was dying. "I'm not afraid to die my darling. But I want to live. I cannot bear to think of my babies alone in this world without their mother."

Searching clumsily for something comforting to say, Theodore told her, "Those who go are happier than those they leave behind."

Maintaining her spirit of humor, she painfully replied, "Ha Ha I know you will be more miserable than I am no matter where I go—or whether I go at all."

When it was nearly her time, her strength waning, she looked into Theodore's eyes and said with a weak death whisper, "I love you darling."

Ninety-six hours after John Konapeck shot her, Ariminta Hunsaker Burmester died. The bullet that entered at her hip likely tore open some part of her intestine without severing any major blood vessels, otherwise she would have died much sooner than four days. Initially the wound would have caused peritonitis, an infection of the membrane which lines the inside of the abdomen called the peritoneum. Without modern medical intervention that infection likely spread to the blood stream. She would have experienced excruciating abdominal pain, nausea and vomiting. The infection would have caused fever and chills. As her blood pressure fell from the septic infection her heart rate would have increased to compensate. Eventually she would have succumbed to shock. Her blood pressure would have dramatically dropped and consequently she would not have been able to circulate oxygenated blood to her brain. Finally, all her organs would have shut down and immediate death would have ensued.[75]

Soon after Theodore arrived back in Boise, he asked one of Ariminta's treating physicians, Dr. Bailey, to write Jacob and Emily to tell them of their daughter's injury. When they received the letter Emily immediately packed a bag and rushed to be at her daughter's bedside. Jacob wrote a four-page letter detailing what he knew to Marianne who was living in Iowa at the time. Emily received help from a friend who operated a boat that sailed the Columbia from Portland to the Dalles. He delayed the boat's departure until Emily reached Portland. The boat took her to the Cascades of the Columbia. From there she took a seven-mile train ride around the Cascades where she boarded another boat to the Dalles. Then the trip slowed to a crawl as she transferred to a stage to Boise. Despite the great effort and all of the assistance, she arrived only after Minnie died.

The funeral was immense. Businesses closed and the Supreme Court specially adjourned so that all could attend and "express the great sorrow of [their] community and their sympathy for the bereaved husband and children."[76] James Reynolds wrote a special editorial in memoriam. In it he compared Ariminta to Lucretia, the Roman noblewoman who, after she was raped by

---

[75] I would like to thank Dr. Edward Leis of the Utah Medical Examiner's Office for his description of what likely happened based on the reported injuries.
[76] "Editorial," *Idaho (Boise) Tri-Weekly Statesman*, May 22, 1869, 2.

Sextus Tarquinius, took her own life to maintain her family honor.[77]

> "History tells us that in ancient times a Roman matron was ravished by her husband's dearest friend. It tells us how speedily terrible vengeance was visited upon the head of Tarquin and his descendants by an outraged community. We are told that Lucretia after recounting the particulars of the affair to her husband stabbed herself to the heart because her living might have given rise among her enemies to the suspicion that she had been false to her husband. Shakespeare and Chaucer have eloquently told the story of Lucrese the Chaste in their immortal verse which will survive through all time.
> More noble and more beautiful was the conduct of our lamented friend."[78]

After Ariminta's death Theodore sent a letter to her sister Marianne. Marianne's daughter, then only five years old, later recounted how when Marianne received Theodore's letter she first sat and read it quietly. Then she suddenly sprang to her feet and ran screaming and crying into the yard terrifying her own daughter who had no idea what was happening. Neighbors poured out of their houses and came running at the commotion. Finally, they were able to calm Marianne, which in turn quieted her terrified daughter who was still too young to understand what it meant that her Aunt Minnie had died.[79]

---

[77] Livy, *The History of Early Rome*, Trans. Aubry de Selincourt, (Norwalk: Easton Press, 1988), 91-93.

[78] "Editorial," *Tri-Weekly Statesman*, May 22, 1869, 2.

[79] D'Arcy, "Reminiscences."

After he laid his beloved to rest, Theodore sent his boys to Oregon under the care of his mother-in-law, Emily. Theodore resumed his work but in life he was hopelessly lost.

Of course, the most serious blow was the loss of his beloved. Moreover, he surely felt some responsibility for her death for not heeding Ariminta's concerns about Konapeck. But this loss was compounded by the virtual loss of his children and the complete loss of his home. Every memory of Minnie except a lock of her hair had been reduced to ashes. He told Marianne that, but for his two boys, he would certainly kill himself because he had nothing else for which to live.

Reynolds' memoriam to Ariminta advised Theodore, "'Some griefs are medicinable,' his is not; time alone can assuage his great sorrow,"[80] But grief such as this needs more than just time. Without the love of his life by his side Theodore's life would soon spin out of control.

---

[80] "Editorial," *Tri-Weekly Statesman*, May 22, 1869, 2.

Chapter 4: Into the Abyss

On November 7, 1869 Theodore and his law partner, S. P. Scaniker, were walking along the River Road on the outskirts of Boise discussing the legal points of an important case on which they were working. As they walked out of town, they saw two men also walking side-by-side coming toward them. Theodore recognized one of the two men, Russell B. Morford, with whom he had been close friends up until a few weeks before.

As they passed one another Morford hissed something under his breath. Scaniker did not hear it, but Theodore took exception. Both parties continued walking in opposite directions for a few steps more as Theodore asked Scaniker in a loud voice, whether he saw what Russell had just done. Scaniker replied that he did not. Theodore suddenly whirled about and confronted Russell Morford, "What do you mean by this?"

Russell yelled back at his former friend, "I mean you are a damned son of a bitch!"

Alarmed by this sudden belligerence, both Scaniker and Morford's acquaintance, Daniel Dwight, yelled at the two men to stop. But it was all to no avail as Burmester and Morford drew pistols and began shooting at one another.

It had been less than six months since his beloved had died from a fatal gun shot and now Theodore was involved in what would prove to be a fatal gun fight himself. How did he get into this situation in six short months?

After the fire, Theodore roomed in a boarding house but also spent nights at several other places. He put a bed in his office and resided there on occasion. At other times he stayed briefly at a cabin on his property where Thomas Bevans lived and where Bevans also farmed by shares.[81] On at least one occasion he stayed in a hotel called Hart's Exchange for a period of several weeks when Theodore's landlady was ill.

Hart's Exchange was an important building in Boise during this period. In addition to serving as an apartment house and hotel, the bar was a meeting place for the community. The legislature even met there in 1866-67.[82]

The Hart's Exchange, Boise, Idaho. Image no. 2111, Idaho State Archives.

---

[81] Unless noted otherwise, all facts in this chapter are taken from newspaper accounts of the testimony of the Burmester trial in the *Idaho Tri-Weekly Statesman* Dec. 21, 1869 to Jan. 13, 1870.
[82] Wells, *Idaho, An Illustrated History*, 44.

Alfred Owens took control of Hart's Exchange in February of 1869. Owens came to know Theodore later that year. Not only was Theodore a short-term resident but he was a frequent visitor of Russell and Amanda Morford who moved into the Exchange in the spring of 1869. During that summer, Owens's also observed that Russell very often stepped out to play cards and drink.

By the summer of 1869, Theodore had known Russell Morford for a year or two since both were members of the bar. Russell was a big burly fellow, congenial, but struggled with a nearly irresistible addiction to gambling.[83] He would go on binges and lose much of what he had earned from his law practice. During these binges he would leave his beautiful wife, Amanda, alone at their room in Hart's Exchange. For her part, Amanda craved attention. Because her husband was frequently out, she sought and received attention from a number of male friends including Theodore, her physician, Dr. Partlow, and a certain Colonel Preston among others. There is no evidence available today that any of these relationships was romantic, but at least one contemporary chronicler described Amanda Morford as "flirtatious."[84]

Theodore first met Amanda Morford in mid-July 1869 at Hart's Exchange. Theodore had come to say farewell to a Mrs. Ainselle who was leaving Boise. While at the Exchange he

---

[83] Donaldson, *Idaho of Yesterday*, 206.
[84] Ibid.

stopped in to see Russell Morford with whom he had recently become quite friendly. There, Russell introduced Theodore to his wife.

When Theodore met Amanda Morford, Theodore was still emotionally rocked from the loss of his beloved Ariminta. After all, in mid-July when he first met Amanda, it had only been a month and a half since his wife's violent death. Frequently, spells of melancholia would reduce him to incapacitating fits of crying. On one such occasion soon after Theodore first met Amanda, Russell let himself into Theodore's office. There he found Theodore lying on his bed crying. Russell, concerned about Theodore's depressed state, invited him to his rooms at Hart's Exchange. Russell promised Amanda would lift his mood by singing and playing her guitar.

As Theodore's relationship grew closer to both Russell and Amanda, he frequently visited their apartment at all times of the day. During the two to three weeks Theodore lived at Hart's Exchange while his landlady recuperated, likely sometime between July 5 and September 2, Theodore often ate with Russell in the hotel and returned to the Morfords' rooms to hear Amanda play and sing.

That same summer Amanda suffered from some lingering malady of her own that at times left her bed-ridden for extended periods. Dr. Partlow diagnosed a "mental problem." It seems likely her mental problem was depression, and perhaps the deterioration of her marriage and her husband's gambling contributed to her condition.

Earlier that year Theodore had engaged a Mr. Paxton to construct a granary for his ranch. Sometime, probably in late July he decided to check on Paxton's progress and mentioned to Russell his intent to take a buggy ride out to the sight.

Theodore's friend responded by asking Theodore to take Amanda with him to the ranch. "Madam is not very well, and a ride would do her good, provided you don't go when the sun is too hot—say after four o'clock. I am not able to take her out riding much. I am not doing any business here yet and can't afford it."[85]

Theodore agreed and so Amanda rode out with him to his ranch. They stopped near Bevans' place and Theodore asked Bevans for some buttermilk. Theodore left Amanda at the buggy while he inspected the granary.

However, by the time Bevans made it out to the buggy with the buttermilk, it was Mrs. Paxton and Russell Morford he saw by the buggy. He then saw Theodore off in the woods about 300 yards away with Amanda. It is not exactly clear how Mrs. Paxton and Russell Morford got there, but it seems likely they came by separate buggy.

Theodore took Amanda into the woods to show her where he and Ariminta had taken their last ride together the weekend before her murder. When they left, Theodore drove Amanda in the

---

[85] "The Burmester Trial!" *Idaho (Boise) Tri-Weekly Statesman*, Jan. 8, 1870.

buggy about a mile up the Dry Creek Road, the opposite direction from Boise, to show her, "the view of the river and the meanderings of the river and the grain fields and the scenery which she appreciated very much."[86] After they had ridden a mile up the road Theodore turned the buggy around and returned to Boise.

Perhaps a week or so later, likely while Theodore was staying at Hart's Exchange, Theodore stood in front of the hotel in the late afternoon when a friend by the name of Briggs came up to him and asked, "Don't you want to take a ride up to the Warm Springs?"

Theodore replied, "Yes if you will take my friend along."[87]

When Briggs replied in the affirmative, Theodore went and found Amanda and asked if she would like to join him and Briggs. Amanda asked her husband if she could go, and Russell readily assented. Theodore and Amanda left the apartment and went downstairs to meet Briggs. They were joined by two other men as well, Mr. Tyne and Joe Davis. The party reached Warm Springs and Tyne, Theodore and Amanda climbed up on a rock precipice that presented a spectacular view of the whole valley below. The three of them sat down on the rock and talked for fifteen to twenty minutes as they looked out from the vista.

---

[86] Ibid.
[87] Ibid.

Finally, Theodore, Amanda and Tyne climbed back down, and the five friends rode back into town together.

It was sometime soon after the trip to Warm Springs that Amanda was struck low by the physical or mental ailment that left her bed ridden.[88] Throughout her ailment Theodore and others continued to visit her frequently. On one occasion, Russell asked Theodore to visit so that he, Russell, could go out. Reluctantly, Theodore agreed and cut short a run he had planned with Major Romily Foote so that he could spell his friend. That night Alfred Owens noticed Theodore visiting with Amanda alone in her room. Though the door was open, Owens thought Theodore's presence in the bedroom with this attractive young married woman unseemly. Later, neighbors, George Greathouse and his wife, came calling to visit Amanda. Greathouse brought the ill woman fresh peaches. He, like Owens, thought Theodore and Amanda's un-chaperoned proximity to one another disquieting. Theodore stayed on that night after the Greathouses left because Russell had not returned. Indeed, he later complained that Morford did not return until after midnight.

By late August 1869, Theodore agreed to sell his ranch, including the property on which Thomas Bevans lived, to John Hailey. Theodore told Russell Morford early in September that he intended to ride out to the property and finalize the transfer. Russell asked Theodore to take Amanda with him for the ride and

---

[88] The timing of Amanda's illness is not expressly stated in the newspaper accounts of the testimony, but this sequence seems most reasonable to me.

Theodore agreed. Theodore and Amanda met John Hailey at the ranch and in the presence of Bevans, Theodore passed the title to Hailey. After completing their business, Theodore left with Amanda. Bevans watched, grimfaced as Theodore and Amanda took yet a third route back to Boise, this time on the Bluff road, not opposite Boise like Dry Creek Road, but still more circuitous than the main road. After the sale, Bevans was forced to leave. Disgruntled, Bevans felt Theodore had not treated him fairly in the ranch transaction. About the indirect route on which he drove Amanda home, Theodore later claimed it was only a mile longer and not as dusty as the main road.

Around September 1, 1869, and apparently not long after this last trip to the ranch, Theodore was sitting in Russell Morford's apartment in Hart's Exchange when Russell confided to him that Amanda had asked for a separation. According to Theodore, Morford told him that he suspected Colonel Preston was encouraging his wife to leave him. He ominously warned that he "would murder the damn son of a bitch."[89] The two men were interrupted when Amanda entered the room.

Theodore broke the ice and said, "This is new to me. I am told you are going to separate. Is there anything I can do for you? If there is I will do it."[90]

According to Theodore, Amanda then said to Russell that they were old enough and mature enough to avoid scandal. So, she

---

[89] Ibid.
[90] Ibid.

encouraged him not to fight the divorce and complete the legal action as quietly as possible.

Russell conceded this point, at least while still in Amanda's presence. According to Theodore, he offered to deal directly with her lawyer as soon as she found herself one.

Amanda turned to Theodore and asked him to represent her in the divorce against Theodore's friend! Displaying remarkably poor judgment, Theodore agreed to represent her in the divorce only moments after Russell had threatened to kill the man he suspected of encouraging it. Theodore then claimed that he and Russell quietly walked down to his office to discuss the terms of the divorce.

Amanda immediately moved out of Hart's Exchange on that same day. On the surface, Russell continued the façade of the concerned but reasonable spouse by making arrangements for Amanda to stay with Ben Drew and his wife. Deep down however, Russell was beside himself. He continued to call on Amanda and to demand she return with him. She quickly tired of his stalking and harassing her and on September 8 while at Drew's house with Mrs. Drew alone, she sent a messenger to John Hailey that she wished to speak with him. When he arrived, Mrs. Drew left the room and Amanda told Hailey that she was serious about divorcing Russell and yet he continued to harass her. She asked Hailey to intercede on her behalf and beseech her husband to cease and desist from contacting her.

For a short time, Hailey avoided committing to any course of action, so Amanda continued to plead with him. Finally, he reluctantly relented and stood up to leave. When Hailey reached the door, he saw Russell in the street coming directly to the house and Hailey warned her that Russell was on his way. Hailey went out to the street to greet Russell and could tell immediately he was angry and ready to take some action. Hailey noted that Russell was red-faced, and even more frightening, kept his hand in his pocket on what Hailey suspected was a pistol. Only when Hailey reached out to shake Russell's hand did he withdraw his hand from his pocket.

"What in thunder does all this trouble mean between you and your wife?" asked Hailey.

"I don't know, can you do anything for me?" Russell replied.

"I don't know Judge, I don't know whether I can or not. Your wife sent for me some time ago, and I have just been talking to her. She seems to be very much out of humor with you, says you have treated her very badly and says she don't want to see you," Hailey explained.

"What do you think about it?" Russell asked, full of anguish.

"I don't know but she seems to be very much out of humor. I would let her rest a day or so and see if she don't [sic] think better of it," Hailey offered.

Hailey then noticed Theodore walking down the side of the street from the same direction Russell had just come. Theodore stopped next to a wagon parked between he and where Russell and Hailey stood.

Russell Morford looked at John Hailey and demanded, "I want to see my wife this evening John."

Likely after a moment's pause Hailey replied, "All right, go ahead if you want to see her."

Russell walked past Hailey and went through the gate to the front door of the Drew residence. At the same time Hailey also saw Burmester proceed to a side gate and through the side door of the same house and he knew there would be trouble.

Somehow word reached Ben Drew, who was at "Rigg's Corner," that trouble was brewing at his home and so he made his way there.

Meanwhile, after Hailey watched Russell Morford and Theodore Burmester enter by different doors he turned and walked slowly south away from the house. He stopped when he saw Theodore come back out. Theodore jogged to catch up to him. Breathless more from excitement than exertion, Theodore said, "Morford has come down here, and says he is going to take his wife up and sleep with her to night [sic] or raise hell."

At first Hailey did not reply. He thoughtfully considered his options. He wanted to go and leave this tawdry affair behind. After all, he didn't have a dog in this fight. But Amanda seemed to have a magical pull on all the men in Fort Boise. Finally, Hailey said, "I guess I will go back and set down in the parlor and if there is any muss kicked up I will try and stop it."

Hailey and Burmester returned to the house and sat in the parlor. Ben Drew arrived home and walked past Hailey and Burmester and up to the bedroom where he found both Russell and Amanda. Drew sat down beside Amanda on the bed. He listened as Russell tried unsuccessfully to get Amanda to leave and take a walk with him. She steadfastly refused to go with him, but he ignored her answer and continued pleading with her to leave.

"Ten-thousand times I have been on my knees to you and you have shoved me away, and now it is my turn," she concluded with emphasis.

Recognizing that he had lost this round Russell vowed, "I will kill the man who marries her," referring to Amanda.

During the hour or so Russell, Amanda, and Ben Drew spent in the bedroom John Hailey and Theodore Burmester had been joined by George Coe. As Russell, followed by Amanda and Ben Drew, walked into the dining room he shouted at Amanda, "I will take a double-barrel shot gun and kill the man you marry!"

Coe, followed by Hailey and Burmester, moved into the dining room at the sound. Hailey scolded Russell for his comment, saying, "Judge, there is no use of using any such language here."

Russell did not reply, instead he walked silently past Hailey out the dining room door to the porch.

Amanda walked back into the bedroom and burst into tears. John Hailey and George Coe were affected by her sobs and left Russell and went into the bedroom to try to console her.

Russell walked back to an open window where Ben Drew and Theodore Burmester were standing and called out to Amanda, "Amanda are you determined in pursuing the course you have stated to me?"

"Yes Judge, we are done forever!" came her tearful reply.

John Hailey did not like Russell's angry facial expression he directed at Amanda in response. He then turned to Coe and said, "Let's get out of here and not stand here like a lot of fools."[91]

As John Hailey and George Coe came out into the dining room, Russell was attempting to come back through the dining room door into the house. Ben Drew blocked his path and held him by the arm and said, "Morford, I don't want you to come into my house ever again!"

"You damned son of a bitch!" Morford snarled back at Drew.

Theodore stepped forward and said, "You ought to be ashamed of yourself." Then holding up his index finger and waving it back and forth he said, "Nobody but a dirty pup would want to crowd into a man's house that didn't want him anyhow."

---

[91] It is interesting that Hailey claimed offense at Russell's facial expressions after he had previously uttered such violent threats. Certainly, they had some impact as well. It is also interesting to note the foreshadowing that seemingly insignificant words and facial expressions could set these Boise men into a violent outburst.

"What are you chipping in about?" Russell asked Theodore.

"When I met you on Main Street Judge, you told me that 'you were going to come down here and raise hell with her if you didn't get her to go to the hotel with you.' [A]nd I said, 'You are not going to do anything discreditable are you?' [A]nd you said you were not. And here you are raising hell and using the most opprobrious epithets against the man who owns this house."

"You don't have anything to do with this affair you son of a bitch!" Russell spat in reply.

"I am doing for Mrs. Morford just what I would do for you under similar circumstances if you were to ask me," said Theodore.

Russell reached into his pocket and cocked his pistol. George Coe stepped forward at that point and warned him that if he persisted in this conduct, he would shoot Russell himself.

Then John Hailey stepped up to Theodore's right side and fearing "the prospects were very good for a row" and in an attempt to prevent it said to Russell, "Judge, don't you draw your pistol! I give you my word if there is any shooting done here, I will take a hand in it myself. Stop this now right away!"

"John I would not have any trouble with you if you would knock me down and stomp on me, I would not resent it," Russell said, backing down.

"I don't know whether you would or not. Judge, I never mis-treated you in my life, but I didn't like the way you met me in the street—you had your hand on your pistol, did you not?"

"Yes I did John."

"What occasion had you for meeting me with your hand on your pistol?"

"I had none, John, but I was mad and vexed, and did not know who was my friend and who was not."

"Well, Judge don't you never meet me that way again, but let us stop this thing now, and go with me and that will end this muss."

"All right," said Russell.

John Hailey took Russell Morford by the arm and he and George Coe walked him towards Hart's Exchange, thus diffusing the tense standoff.

The following night Russell came to John Hailey and asked that Amanda be allowed to move into Hailey's home instead of staying at Ben Drew's. While Amanda remained at Ben Drew's house, Russell asserted, "She is surrounded with an influence that is all against me." Furthermore, Russell claimed that Theodore was trying to induce Amanda to leave him. "If you will allow her to come and stop at your house she would be away from that influence, and I think in a short time she would be willing to come back and live with me."

Hailey replied, "Judge, I must say that you are a little different from what I think I would be if my wife wanted to leave me. I would let her go."

"I can not give her up. I am helpless without her," Russell said as he began to cry. "So far as her virtue is concerned, I think she is as pure as the driven snow, but unfortunately for me I am without money, and all this influence is all against me. If I had money I would be all right. Can she stay with you John?"

"Judge to tell you the truth, what I think about the matter, I think you have acted very badly for the last two years. I don't pretend to know or say anything about you or your wife, but of course your drinking and gambling is very bad. My opinion is unless you change your course, your wife will not live with you again."

"If you will let her come to your house and stay, I will change my course and never drink another drop or play another card. I can then go away satisfied. [I will] go away and establish myself in business somewhere else. I will pay you to take care of her. If I cannot make any money at my profession, I will make it chopping cord wood."

"So far as pay is concerned you need not trouble yourself about that," he replied. Then Hailey added, "I never took a lady to my house without consulting my wife." Then he explained that if his wife approved Amanda could stay at his house.

Hailey left to conduct some business so that by the time he arrived home, Russell had already been there and obtained Mrs.

Hailey's approval for Amanda to stay with the Haileys. John Hailey went to Ben Drew's and Amanda agreed to change her residence yet again. While meeting with Amanda, John Hailey asked her to reconsider her decision to divorce Russell. Amanda insisted that her mind was made up. To which Hailey urged her to change her choice of legal counsel. John explained that Theodore Burmester had recently lost his wife and was therefore young and eligible. This would inevitably have the townsfolk spreading rumors, so he encouraged her to hire a married man as her lawyer so as not to encourage scandalous rumors.

Hailey arranged a brief meeting between Russell and Amanda when the stagecoach arrived to take him to Oneida County to start his new life. Russell was sad and wiped tears from his eyes as he bid her farewell.

During the time that Russell was in Oneida, Theodore and Amanda were seen in public together only once—the horse races in October. Even then, Theodore and Amanda only sat together for some of the races, as she had arrived and subsequently left with someone else. Nothing else in the drama was reported while Russell was away in Oneida. But when Russell returned sometime around the end of October or the first of November, the dispute between Russell and Theodore had for some reason grown ugly.

On the day Russell Morford returned from Oneida County, Joseph Huston was walking from the courthouse with Judge Lewis when they crossed paths with Russell. The men greeted Russell, shook hands and happily asked him how his business was going in Oneida. Russell replied briefly and Huston pressed him with follow-up questions. Russell hesitated and his facial expression suddenly turned malevolent and his eyes focused on something beyond Huston and Lewis. Huston repeated his question and when Russell did not answer he cast a quick glance over his shoulder to see what he was looking at. What he saw was Theodore Burmester who had just emerged from his office and was walking toward the courthouse. Russell remained mute, transfixed on Burmester until the latter entered the court side-door. Huston and Lewis later agreed that Russell Morford's expression was "devilishly wicked."

Chapter 5: "I mean you are a damned son of a bitch!"

<u>November 6</u>

Russell Morford and Theodore Burmester next met on the evening of November 6 at Hart's Exchange. Theodore had purchased two tickets to the St. Clair lecture scheduled for that night. He invited Mrs. Drew to the lecture as his guest and had gone to Hart's Exchange to retrieve his tickets. As he left the dining room, he encountered Russell who, according to Theodore, suddenly grasped his pistol in order to pull it out. Another person entered the office and Russell loosened his grip and Theodore took the opportunity to evade him and escaped into the bar where he saw John Hultz. John Hultz had known Russell Morford since 1852. On the other hand, by November of 1869 he had known Theodore Burmester for only about two months. Theodore walked directly to the card table where Hultz was sitting. Moments later Russell entered the bar and walked to the stove near Hultz and Theodore. Russell gave Theodore a menacing scowl. Worried for his safety, Theodore got up and sat on the other side of Hultz so that Hultz was between him and Russell. Hultz then noticed Russell for the first time and greeted him. Russell's response was curt and caused Hultz to ask Theodore what was wrong with Morford. Then Russell abruptly stood up and walked outside to the porch where he paced back and forth three or four times before leaving.

Later, Robert Irwin claimed to also have been in Hart's Exchange at that same time on November 6. He denied that Russell appeared menacing and that Theodore ever changed his position. However, he admitted he heard Hultz ask why Russell Morford was so surly, but he could give no explanation as to why Hultz would even ask the question. Hultz, for his part, denied seeing Irwin in Hart's Exchange that night.

After Russell left, Theodore met Mrs. Drew and took her to the lecture. When the lecture ended, he escorted Mrs. Drew home and was on his way to his office when he suddenly saw Russell standing in the shadows in front of his office on Eighth Street. Theodore was surprised and scared. Nervously he backed down the street, never looking away from Russell. Just as Theodore began backing down the street Russell walked up a nearby alley. Theodore turned onto Idaho Street from which he was able to see Russell emerge from the alley on to Seventh Street and enter Hart's Exchange.

Theodore ran to his office where he slammed the door, considering his options as his heart pounded in his chest. Believing he was likely to be murdered, Theodore decided to call on Henry E. Prickett, who also happened to be his lawyer. Theodore left his office again. Nervously looking over his shoulder in the cold evening air as he sneaked down the dark street to Henry Pricket's office.

Once he arrived, Theodore explained to Prickett what had just occurred. One can imagine him trying to describe the events to

Prickett in a rush of words tangled with fear, gasping for breath, trying to explain how he thought Russell Morford was going to ambush him on a dark street. Theodore said, "You know all about the circumstances of this matter. [Do you think] Morford has any right to be hunting me down in this way? What would you do under these circumstances?"

"I would arm myself," said Prickett, "and I would defend myself."

"I have no security, he has," replied Theodore.

"I have one," Prickett responded.

"Will you lend it to me?"

"I will," answered Prickett.

But in the end, Theodore left that night without Prickett's gun. Apparently Prickett kept the gun in the house where he was staying. He did not wish to disturb his landlady at that late hour, so he delivered the gun to Theodore the next morning. Theodore also later claimed to have gone to Prickett's office with the secondary purpose of drafting or updating his will. However, it seems he left without accomplishing that either. Despite still being unarmed Theodore was able to make it home safely to his office and went to bed.

November 7

The next morning Theodore was back in his office preparing a brief of authorities for a case he and his partner, S. P. Scaniker, were working on. By the time Scaniker arrived, Theodore had the cases strewn around the office because he had already been feverishly studying them. The two had parted the night before in disagreement on a particular point of law, but by the next morning Scaniker had changed his mind. Nevertheless, they both wanted to consult two more experienced lawyers, Frank Ganahl and Joseph Rosborough.

Scaniker and Theodore then left their office to go speak to their elder colleagues. Outside, they happened to notice that the two men they sought were walking down Seventh Street away from them, so they set off to catch them. Theodore saw Ganahl and Rosborough cross Main Street and then cross a little foot bridge over the ditch on Market Street. The two elder lawyers then turned onto Market Street itself. Theodore told Scaniker that they must be taking Rosborough's routine walk out to Jacob's Mill. Theodore and Scaniker hesitated at Main Street trying to decide what to do. Finally, they chose not to pursue Ganahl and Rosborough, and instead of continuing on Seventh Street to Market, they fatefully turned and walked down toward the river on Main Street.

Meanwhile, earlier that same morning, a man named Daniel Dwight walked into Hart's Exchange to meet with his friend Russell Morford. Daniel had only recently come to Boise from Umatilla County, Oregon and did not know either Scaniker or Burmester. So of course, he had no idea that Russell Morford had even been friends with Theodore Burmester, much less that their previously warm friendship had devolved into a grotesque hatred. Moreover, he could never have imagined the violent end their relationship would come to that morning.

Russell suggested to Daniel that they take a walk and discuss their business. They too walked out Main Street, just ahead, but out of sight of Theodore and Scaniker. Daniel and Russell had gone about one half mile when Russell said that they had walked far enough so they turned around and began to retrace their steps. As they walked back down stream, paralleling the river, Daniel was on the left and Russell on his right, to the inside of the road.

Coming up the road Theodore was on the right, on the inside of the road while Scaniker walked on his left to the outside of the road. Thus, as the two parties approached one another Scaniker and Daniel Dwight were on either side of the road while the former friends turned rivals passed next to each other.

As they passed, neither Dwight nor Scaniker heard any comments or noises from Theodore or Russell. However, Theodore claimed that as they passed one another, Russell hissed something at him between clenched teeth shaking his head and partially removing his gun from his holster. Once they had taken perhaps ten to fifteen steps after passing, Theodore grabbed at Scaniker's jacket with this left hand and asked, "Scaniker, did you see these motions?"

To which, Scaniker replied, "No, I don't want to see them."

Theodore suddenly turned around and called out, "Judge Morford what do you mean by all this?"

Russell stopped and abruptly turned to face Theodore. "I mean you are a damned son of a bitch!"

Scaniker, who by this time had also stopped and turned, began to yell, "Stop! Stop!"

By this time both men had drawn their revolvers.[92] Scaniker still hoped that both men would hold their fire. Daniel too yelled, "For God's sake, gentlemen don't shoot!" He then turned to get away from Russell's side while Scaniker ran to get away from Theodore.

What happened next became the central issue of the dispute in the prosecution that followed. Both Theodore and Scaniker insisted that Russell fired first and only then did Theodore return fire. Indeed, according to Theodore and Scaniker, Theodore exclaimed, "Don't you see he shot at me!"[93] Daniel Dwight initially claimed in his affidavit at the time that when he saw both men armed and "about to shoot I turned to get out of the way, while I was doing this two shots were fired, very close together. I do not know which one fired first."[94] He was certain that Theodore fired three shots but thought Russell only fired two but might have fired three. Theodore and Scaniker said that

---

[92] Aff. of S.P. Scaniker, Nov. 7,1869.

[93] Quote is from Theodore Burmester's testimony. S. P. Scaniker testified that Theodore said something that he could not hear before he returned fire. Daniel Dwight claimed that Theodore made this protestation about Russell firing first only after Russell lay prostrate on the road.

[94] Aff. of D.P. Dwight, Nov. 7, 1869.

Russell fired three shots. In any event, no shot hit its mark until Theodore's third which hit Russell Morford on the forehead above his right eye and he fell forward on his hands and knees.

Daniel Dwight immediately ran to his friend and knelt by his side. He called out to him "Judge Morford!" However, Russell just lay there barely breathing; the bullet had crashed through Russell's skull and torn into his brain. Both Theodore and Scaniker ran to the ditch on the side of the road and ran past Russell and Daniel Dwight back toward town. When they were nearly out of ear-shot Daniel hollered to Scaniker, urging him to send help; a wagon and a doctor.

Theodore followed closely behind Scaniker. Partially out of fear and partially out of anger at what had just transpired, Scaniker abruptly stopped and scolded Theodore for following him and told him to go away. When he continued to follow, Scaniker again "told him in the most peremptory manner to keep away from me—perhaps I might get shot in this fuss and not have anything to do with it." At that, Theodore sheepishly left Scaniker behind and walked alone into town.

Daniel Dwight stayed by Russell Morford's side and waited, hoping that help would arrive soon. At first the prospect of help arriving quickly (at least by 1870 standards) seemed promising when not long after Scaniker left, an unidentified man rode up on horseback. Daniel asked him to go into town and send help. He agreed and quickly rode off. Another man rode past soon thereafter, followed by several men on foot whom Daniel described as Spaniards. Next, a man named Agnew rode by and still no help had arrived. Daniel pleaded with him to send help. Agnew returned to town and came back with a wagon, whereupon Russell, only barely alive, was loaded into the wagon and taken into town.

Dr. Wagner, who had so recently treated the ultimately fatal wounds of Ariminta, rushed to see him and met him about one mile above town according to his affidavit. The ball he said, penetrated the forehead on the right side, "producing an extensive fracture of the frontal bone from which brain substance and blood flowed freely."[95] There was not much Wagner could do for him with the medical understanding of the typical physician of 1869. At the time, he thought the wound fatal and he was correct as Russell Morford died some fifteen to sixteen hours after Dr. Wagner first saw him.

At the scene Theodore had lamented that "scarcely have I got my head out of one trouble until here I am in another!" After separating from Scaniker he walked back to town alone and went straight back to the office of his lawyer and friend, Henry Prickett. There he told Prickett what had just transpired.

The following afternoon, Monday November 8, 1869, Theodore Burmester walked into the office of James Reynolds, at the Idaho Tri-Weekly Statesman, and declared that "he wished [Reynolds] to hear the correct story in regard to the affair."

_____

[95] Aff. of Dr. C. Wagner, Nov. 7, 1869.

Reynolds answered that he "was anxious to hear it." The story that Theodore told Reynolds concerning the events was the same as that which Theodore subsequently testified to. However, Reynolds claimed that Theodore made several boasts to him in this conversation which Theodore later denied making. Reynolds said that Theodore told him that he thought Russell Morford was bent on killing him. Thus, fear drove him to Prickett's office to make out his will the night before the killing. In his testimony Theodore agreed with this but departed from this version when Reynolds claimed Theodore said he had even thought of preemptively bringing the conflict to a conclusion by "putting on my hunting suit and taking my gun and coming into town or appear to come into town, hunt up Morford, call to me, and ask him what he meant by his conduct or his threats, and if he made a draw or made a motion to shoot him down or take him on the wing." Reynolds also claimed that Theodore had boasted, "I don't feel as if I was guilty of any crime any more than if I had shot a dog in the street."

After talking to James Reynolds, Theodore surrendered to the sheriff and he was booked into jail. Justice of the Peace A. Haas listened to the arguments of Joseph Roseborough who appeared on Theodore's behalf. He denied the motion to release but granted bail in the amount of $3,000.[96] However, the Idaho

---

[96] *People v. Theodore Burmester*, Tr. of Justice Court Docket Nov. 8, 1869.

World later reported that when he was indicted, he asked for and was denied bail.[97]

The Trial

The case of the People of the United States in the Territory of Idaho vs. Theodore Burmester was a cause célèbre.[98] There were only a little over a dozen lawyers in Boise at the time.[99] Theodore moved in the highest circles and, a fortiori, so did Russell Morford. Moreover, each side made the most salacious and scandalous claims regarding Amanda Morford and Theodore as well as Russell. As a consequence, the readers of the Idaho World and the Idaho Tri-Weekly Statesman hung on every word the papers reported.

The Idaho World reported on November 18, 1869 that the Grand Jury for Ada County indicted Theodore Burmester for murder in the first degree. On Wednesday, December 15, less than a month later, the judge and the sheriff selected the names of one hundred men and then drew sixty of them to sit as the venire from which Theodore's jury would be drawn.[100] The next morning the trial began.

The judge refused to allow the newspapers to report the content of the witnesses' testimony before the jury was

---

[97] "Fatal Affray," *Idaho (Idaho City) World*, Nov. 10, 1869, 2; "Indicted," *Idaho World*, Nov. 18, 1869, 2.

[98] "The Burmester Trial!" *Tri-Weekly Statesman*, Dec. 21, 1869. "Never before in the criminal history of the Territory has a case awakened so much interest in the public mind."

[99] Donaldson, *Idaho of Yesterday*, 203.

[100] "City and County," *Idaho (Idaho City) World*, Dec. 30, 1869, 3.

sequestered to deliberate. Thursday, December 23 the jury was charged, and the lawyers argued their cases. On that day the Idaho Tri-Weekly Statesman ran the first installment in a series with extracts of each of the witnesses' testimony beginning with the Government's first witness. The public interest in the trial was so great that the Idaho Statesman continued to report an extract of each witness' testimony with each issue until they had published the extract of all witnesses, both the government's and the Defense's, including rebuttal witnesses.[101] The Idaho Statesman published its last installment of the trial testimony on January 13, 1870, long after the jury rendered their verdict late on December 23, 1869.

Major Romily E. Foote. Image no. 111-B, Idaho State Archives.

---

[101] *Tri-Weekly Statesman*, Dec. 28, 1869, 2, column 2. "Though the Burmester trial is ended we continue the publication of the testimony believing that the hideous moral deformity it develops is a needed lesson. The disclosures to be made in our next issue are almost too brutal for belief."

The lead prosecutor on the case was none other than Theodore's running friend, Romily Foote. Assisting him was E. D. "Ned" Holbrook. Ned Holbrook, a Democrat, had served as Idaho Territory's representative to Congress from 1864 until he lost his bid for a third term in 1868. Though he originally haled from Ohio, he surrounded himself with Southern ex-patriots and faithfully served their causes in Congress.[102]

The defense team had no less than five attorneys (not counting the defendant). What is remarkable is that of the thirteen lawyers who were practicing in Boise in 1869, twelve of them were in some way involved with the trial.[103] One was the decedent and one the defendant. Five were defense attorneys and two prosecutors. Three more, Scaniker, Prickett, and Huston, were witnesses.

The roll of lead counsel for the defense was shared by the two senior lawyers Burmester and Scaniker sought on that fateful November morning: Joseph Roseborough and the corpulent Frank Ganahl. Roseborough appears to have been the legal mind of the two, while Ganahl, the renowned southern orator, was the voice.[104]

---

[102] Donaldson, *Idaho of Yesterday*, 144.
[103] Ibid., 203. Although Donaldson claims there were only 13 practicing lawyers, he names more than that and does not mention 2 of Burmester's defense attorneys named in the Idaho World.
[104] Ibid., 203; "The Burmester Trial," *Idaho World*, Dec. 30, 1869, 2.

Frank E. Ganahl. Image no. 249-15, Idaho State Archives.

In addition, the defense was assisted by John R. McBride, a Republican, who had been the Idaho representative in Congress preceding Holbrook from 1860 until 1864. In 1865 he had been appointed a territorial judge by President Lincoln and served the citizens of the Territory in that capacity until 1868. At the time of the trial he was a general agent for the Treasury Department, supervising the building of the United States Assay Office in Boise.[105] Two other lawyers, P. E. Edmonson and Major E. H. McDaniel also assisted the defense.[106]

The judge assigned to the case after Theodore's indictment was Judge David Noggle. Judge Noggle came to Idaho from Wisconsin, an appointee of President Grant. He came with a

---

[105] Donaldson, *Idaho of Yesterday*, 197.
[106]"The Burmester Trial," *Idaho World*, Dec. 30, 1869, 2.

reputation for incompetence and was immediately resented as a carpetbagger.[107] Noggle was old, around seventy years, when he first assumed the territorial bench in 1869. He was fairly tall, being around six feet in height. He had a burly body set upon two spindly legs. He had thick gray hair on his overly large head with eyes that drooped down and narrowed at the cheek. To match his disagreeable temperament both on and off the bench he possessed an annoying high-pitched voice.[108]

The thrust of the prosecution's case was two-fold. First, that Theodore was the aggressor and had fired first. The prosecution sought to establish that there was a total of only five shots fired. It was an undisputed fact that Theodore had fired three shots in a general exchange where each of the combatants alternated firing at the other and that Theodore had fired the last shot which caused the death of Morford. Thus, logically, if indeed five shots were fired then Theodore had to have shot first.

The second part of the prosecution's case was that Theodore had struck up an inappropriate if not illicit relationship with Amanda. Motivated by his desire to have her for his own, Theodore baited Russell into a confrontation so that he could kill him under the pretext of self defense.

The first witness for the prosecution was Daniel Dwight. He was a dramatic witness who was present for the shooting and watched in horror as his friend was shot dead. However, under

---

[107] Donaldson, *Idaho of Yesterday*, 191.
[108] Ibid.

cross examination he conceded that he might have been mistaken as to who shot first.

The prosecution next called Moses Watkins who was on the River road. He testified that he heard the first two shots in succession and that the first shot whizzed by him. Though he did not see the first shots, he watched as the men continued to fire. Theodore Burmester was the further of the two away from him and therefore, he surmised, had to have been the first to fire.

The next two witnesses were Moses' father, Simeon Watkins and an E. Lopez. They each testified that they were at their respective houses and that they each saw Theodore Burmester fire first.

Dr. Wagner was the next witness called to the stand. He testified that Morford died from a gun shot wound to the head. Following the physician's testimony, both parties read into the record as a stipulation that a witness named Holbrook[109] found a pistol on the ground next to Morford's body. He collected that pistol and passed it on to a witness named Gumbert who in-turn passed it on to Sheriff Branstetter in the same condition in which Holbrook originally found it. With that, the court adjourned for the day.

On Friday morning the 17th of December the prosecution called the County Recorder, Wood Flippen, who testified that

---

[109] It is unclear whether this is the prosecutor Ned, or some other man named Holbrook. Perhaps it was the prosecutor and the agreement was reached to keep the lawyer from becoming a witness.

Russell Morford had come to his office on the morning of November 7. Shortly after Russell left, Flippen stepped out of his office and saw Burmester and Scaniker leave their office. Later that morning, he met Sheriff Branstetter who told him about the shooting. They walked together a short distance when Theodore came around the corner and walked up to the Sheriff and said, "You can consider me under your charge."

According to Flippen, Sheriff Branstetter placed Theodore under arrest. Theodore then told the Sheriff he wished to speak to Roseborough and Ganahl. Despite wisely demanding the assistance of counsel he stupidly proceeded to tell Flippen how he had shot Russell and even showed them the short revolver he had used, removing it from his pocket.

After Flippen, the prosecutor shifted into the second phase of their case: motive. To begin they called on John Hailey to recount the events at Ben Drew's residence from September 8. The defense did not have to work very hard to make Russell appear the more violent and menacing one. The prosecution then had Alfred Owens, proprietor of Hart's Exchange, testify that Theodore visited Amanda often and that they were friendlier to one another than he thought appropriate.

Thomas Bevans was the next prosecution witness. He testified to the three times that Theodore came out to the ranch with Amanda Morford. On cross examination however, the defense got Bevans to admit that he and Theodore were no longer on friendly terms after Theodore sold the ranch to John Hailey and was thus biased against him. Further, Bevans had testified on direct examination that Theodore and Amanda had taken various routes home that were more circuitous than necessary and thereby the prosecution inferred that some dalliance had occurred. But on cross examination he was forced to admit that the roads he saw Theodore take also led back to Boise and though longer were less dusty in Summer than the Main Road.

To reinforce the claim that Theodore and Amanda's buggy trips to the country were inappropriate the prosecution called Joseph Davis, the owner of the buggy who drove himself, Theodore, Mr. Tyne and Amanda to Warm Springs. The Defense tried to deflect the tenor of the scandalous assertion by getting Davis to acknowledge that Theodore did not object to Davis inviting Tyne, drawing the inference that the trip was, for Theodore and Amanda, a platonic outing and not a romantic one.

George Greathouse was the government's next witness. He testified concerning the visit he and his wife paid Amanda when she was ill, and that during that visit, he saw Theodore holding her hand. He also told the jury he had seen the pair walking together. The goal of the defense on cross examination was again to show bias, and Greathouse obliged them by admitting that he did not like Theodore.

The testimony of the prosecution's next witness was very strange. A certain G. Quivey testified that he had had a conversation with Theodore one week "before the killing of Morford occurred" during which Theodore said "that Dr. Partlow wished to get Mrs. Morford away from him (Burmester) and out from under his influence; that he wanted her to go to Canyon City and away from him (Burmester) in order that he might marry her himself." I don't know if the testimony is just strange or whether the paper's summary is edited unskillfully. In any event the cross examination was a repeat of the odd direct examination.

Following Quivey, the prosecution followed up with yet another strange witness who only tangentially forwarded their theory of the case. Mr. P. Mace was employed at Agnew's Livery Stable which stood across the street from Theodore's office. He testified on direct examination at length that Russell Morford had stabled his team of horses there but on one day in November had come by at about nine o'clock to tell Mace his man would take the horses and a bail of hay he bought and corral them outside town because the livery stable was too expensive. Almost as an afterthought the prosecution elicited testimony from Mace that Theodore routinely rented buggies from Agnew's and on one or two occasions, he had seen Theodore ride away in a buggy with Amanda Morford. On cross examination the defense ineffectively had the witness reiterate essentially the same testimony.

The next witness the prosecution called to the stand after Mace was the most salacious testimony of the entire trial. At the time of the trial A. J. Vincent was living in Umatilla, Oregon but had been living in Boise during the critical period: July through October 1869. By the Summer of 1869, although he had only lived in Boise a short time, he had known Amanda, Russell and

Theodore for a number of years. His testimony for the prosecution focused on a series of conversations he claimed to have had with Theodore that summer preceding Russell's death.

According to Vincent, Theodore began asking Vincent about Amanda—if he knew her and how long he had known her. At some point, according to Vincent, Theodore asked him what her "general reputation" was.[110] Although by the time of trial he could not remember Theodore's exact words, he testified that Theodore asked him "what [he] thought about her virtue."

Vincent replied to Theodore's inquiry that he thought "that she had always had the reputation of being a very fine lady, except a report that I heard about her at Umatilla."

Theodore inquired whether he knew the details of the report and Vincent replied that he did not; that it was "merely a rumor."

Then, according to Vincent, Theodore asked, "if [he] thought there would be any chance to get any _____ there?"[111]

Vincent said that he replied, "I didn't know, but if I was a moneyed cuss, and rather high toned, I would go after it."

That was all he could remember of that conversation. However, Vincent testified that later Theodore met him near the latter's office and requested his help in a scheme to keep Russell

---

[110] "The Burmester Trial!" *Tri-Weekly Statesman*, Dec. 30, 1869, 2. All quotations regarding the conversation other than Burmester's denial that it occurred are taken from this source.

[111] The newspapers of the time apparently used the underscore as a form of "bleeping" offensive language.

out late gambling so that he could be alone with Amanda. So on two occasions Theodore gave Vincent money to gamble with, twenty dollars the first time and thirty the second, and each time Vincent took Russell out gambling. "Fifty dollars [for Theodore] to satisfy himself," Vincent testified.

The prosecutor asked, "To satisfy himself of what?"

Vincent answered, "Well I supposed to satisfy himself as to her virtues, so I understood it."

Vincent went on to testify that when he next talked to Theodore after the second night of gambling, he told Vincent that "[Vincent] was wrong, that [Vincent] had put it up wrong." Later, on cross examination, Vincent clarified that he "understood [Theodore] to mean that he had been disappointed that he did not 'fetch.'"

Next, Vincent testified that he had two subsequent conversations with Theodore which the prosecution likely hoped would make the Defendant appear ever more paranoid and scheming. Vincent claimed that after Russell had returned to Boise from Oneida, Theodore saw him talking to Russell on the street. Once they separated, Theodore came up to Vincent and questioned Vincent as to what Russell had been saying about him. Finally, Vincent told the jury about yet another conversation he had had with the Defendant. On the 5th of November, two days before the gunfight, Theodore happened to meet up with Vincent where-upon he asked Vincent how Russell was doing. Vincent replied that Russell was a wreck and destitute. Wistfully, he added that if he had the money himself, he would help Russell out. But Theodore, according to Vincent, stubbornly insisted that he would not help Russell though he would help Amanda. The ever-loyal Vincent countered that he would help Russell because he knew that Russell would do the same for him. Vincent claimed that Theodore uncharitably replied, "[I] wouldn't give the d__d s_n of a b__h a cent."

The Defense did not really do anything with Vincent on cross examination. They established that the gambling scheme took place in September and that Vincent believed Russell and Theodore were still close friends at the time. Finally, Vincent said that after the gambling scheme Theodore told Vincent that the Umatilla rumor was wrong, "if ever there was a pure woman on the face of the earth she was one."

The testimony of the next witness for the prosecution was short and simple and returned to the theme that there were five shots and thus Theodore shot first. Frank Babb was in his bed on November 7 when about 10:00 a.m. he heard a single shot from a distance that drew his attention. After the initial shot he heard two shots in quick succession followed by another short delay before two more quick shots.

Ada Chapman and Hector Dow were the next two prosecution witnesses. Chapman lived in a house four or five doors down the street from Theodore's office where she employed Dow. She and Dow each testified that they saw Burmester and Scaniker standing outside their office on the morning of the shooting. But it was Theodore who drew their attention when they heard him cursing and swinging his cane in apparent anger. However, on cross examination they were forced to concede that they could not tell who he was cursing or why. Chapman and Dow then went on about their business only to hear that 30 to 45 minutes later Theodore Burmester had shot Judge Morford.

The prosecution followed up with two very quick witnesses. First, they called H. C. Riggs who merely observed Theodore Burmester and S.P. Scaniker walk up Main Street on the morning of the Seventh. Then about thirty minutes later he was at the Overland Hotel when Scaniker came in and told him that there had been a "terrible affair," and Theodore had shot Russell Morford dead. The Prosecution then followed Riggs with A. Haas, who described the measurements between Theodore's office and Ada Chapman's neighbor's residence and testified that there were no visual obstructions between the two. On cross examination Haas denied that he contributed money to the prosecution of the case but admitted that he solicited money for the cause. Recall that he was the Justice of the Peace who decided custody and bail in the case! He also conceded that he was no friend to Theodore Burmester.

The prosecution was nearing the conclusion of its case-in-chief. At this point they recalled Daniel Dwight for a very strange exchange. Daniel testified that when Morford fell mortally wounded, Theodore said, "There, damn you, take that and see how you like it!" It is strange because they had to recall him to elicit the statement. It is the sort of emotional outburst a prosecutor really strives to get out. Because it only came in after he was recalled at the end of the case it appears to me and probably the jury at the time, as if the prosecution was incompetent with such a gross oversight, or else that the witness was coached. This appearance is especially pronounced because the purported statement fits four-square within the theme of the prosecution's case—that the defendant lusted after Russell Morford's wife and created the very circumstances that caused his death, sort of like David and Uriah. The bumbling continued with this witness when Dwight identified the prosecution's map, stating it appeared to be correct but, refused to confirm whether it was accurate.[112]

The last witness in the prosecution's case was none other than James S. Reynolds, editor of the Idaho Tri-Weekly Statesman and leader of the Boise Vigilante Committee. Reynolds testified to the substance of the interview he had with Theodore on November 8, 1869, the day after the shooting.

The last line of questioning by the prosecution attempted to focus on the second prong of the prosecution's case but ended up being subsumed by the defense theory—that Theodore had merely responded in self defense. Reynolds testified that Theodore told him he feared Russell "Morford had intended to kill him," and

---

[112] A sacred tenet of prosecution is never ask a witness a question you don't know what their answer will be. That is what seems to have happened here. However, I must confess that I have committed the same sin, asking a witness the foundational question whether the exhibit would be helpful in conveying their testimony and they replied, "No."

so he went to see Henry Prickett to make his will the night before the shooting. Due to the stress he felt, Theodore wanted to confront Russell and bring the conflict between he and Russell to an end once and for all.

On cross examination the defense elicited from Reynolds several more times Theodore's fear of Russell which must have seemed reasonable after John Hailey's testimony about the events at Drew's house. However, they too stumbled when Reynolds responded to their questioning by quoting Theodore as having said, "I don't feel as if I was guilty of any crime any more than if I had shot a dog in the street."[113]

And that was the end of the prosecution's case-in-chief.

The Defense

The defense began its case by poking holes in the first prong of the prosecution's case—that Theodore had fired first. The first defense witness was Mr. Jas. H. Slater, a civil engineer who took measurements of the scene in relation to stated locations of some of the prosecution's eyewitnesses and then drew a diagram of the scene. He had men stand in the positions where Russell and Theodore had been when they were shooting at one another and then went to both Simeon Watkins' home and Lopez's home to see what those witnesses would have been able to see. Slater discovered that from Watkins' home it was 1,660 feet to where the dual took place and from the point where Watkins said he was

---

[113] "The Burmester Trial!" *Tri-Weekly Statesman*, Dec. 30, 1869, 2.

standing he would only have been able to see the head of one combatant and the bust of the other. Lopez's residence was 1,480 feet from the scene and his view was a little better; he would have been able to see from the waist up of the down-stream man (Russell at the time of the shooting) and from the thigh up on the up-stream man (Theodore).

The defense next called Sheriff H. C. Branstetter, through whom the defense introduced Russell Morford's Remington pistol, which he had received from George Gumbert at the scene on November 7. When he received the pistol from Gumbert it was covered with dirt and blood and so he could not tell which chambers had recently been fired. However, at the time he received it there were still three chambers charged (loaded) and three that had been discharged!

Next the defense called Hailey Simpson,[114] a firearms expert who had been in the business of repairing firearms for some twenty years. He explained that the rifling in a Remington pistol such as the one Morford used had fewer grooves in the barrel than a Colt like Theodore had. Further, the grooves in the Remington were not as deep nor as tightly curved as the Colt. Simpson explained to the jury that the report of the Remington was louder than the Colt but flat like a shot gun, not sharp like the Colt.

Following Simpson, the defense called their first eyewitness and Theodore's law partner, S. P. Scaniker. His

---

[114] The newspaper print is difficult to read Simpson's first name. Hailey is my best guess.

testimony dealt almost exclusively with the events of the morning of November 7. On both direct and cross examination, he insisted that Russell Morford fired first. He heard the bullet whiz past and then Theodore exclaimed something about Russell shooting at him. He also gave a detailed account of his actions that morning when he arrived at the office and when he and Theodore left to look for Ganahl and Rosborough. Importantly, he denied that the heated argument took place outside his office on the morning of the shooting as Ada Chapman and Hector Dow had testified to during the prosecution's case.

The next two witnesses, William and Julian Neville, were brief witnesses designed to impeach the prosecution witness Simeon Watkins. Watkins had testified that he had been at his home on November 7 when he saw Theodore fire first. However, both William and Julian Neville testified that on November 7 they saw "Old Man Watkins" near Agnew's Stable and heard him say that it was the man coming down river who fired first. The problem for the prosecution was that it was uncontroverted that Russell and Dwight had turned around on their walk and were walking back down stream when they passed Scaniker and Theodore who were walking upriver—making Russell the one who fired first.

The next witness, Antoine Campeas, was staying at the house next to Lopez at the time of the shooting. It is difficult to determine from the newspaper summary the purpose of this witness. He heard the shooting, but it did not distract him from saddling his horse. He noticed Lopez, standing on a stick watching the events and remembered that two of the men who had been at the shooting, later walked past the house one just ahead of the other.

Similarly, the testimony of the subsequent witness, Santos Plas, was perplexing as to its purpose. Like Campeas, a great deal of his testimony had to do with his observations of Lopez and the stick upon which Lopez stood while watching the shooting.

After Campeas and Plas, Henry Prickett took the stand. Prickett testified that he was aware of the "difficulty between Burmester and Morford" generally. When asked how he knew, he replied that Theodore had told him. The defense attorney then attempted to elicit the substance of Theodore's statement and of course the prosecution leaped to their feet and objected, claiming the answer would be hearsay. Judge Noggle sustained the objection and the defense was forced to move on. Prickett was then asked if he had seen Theodore on the evening of November 6, to which, he replied that he had at his office. Again, when asked about the content of the communication the prosecution objected and the judge sustained it. Although it appears to be rather basic hearsay, I can imagine a defense attorney today being successful in getting the statement in when the prosecution had earlier offered Theodore's conversation with Henry Prickett through the testimony of James S. Reynolds. Regardless what argument the defense made at the time, Judge Noggle refused to allow the testimony and the defense gave up in exasperation.

The defense called Joseph Huston next who testified to his chance meeting with Russell upon the latter's return from Oneida about a week before the shooting. This was the encounter where he quoted Judge Lewis' description of Russell Morford's look he gave an unsuspecting Theodore Burmester as "devilishly wicked."

The defense followed with John Hultz who testified about the incident at Hart's Exchange on the evening of November 6 when Theodore came in and joined him at a card table. When Russell came in shortly thereafter Theodore changed positions. Russell's curt reply to Hultz's greeting caused him to ask Theodore what was bothering him. Before he could testify to Theodore's response the prosecution objected and the court sustained that objection, again on the grounds of hearsay.

E. C. Sterling, the next witness, testified that the day before the incident at Ben Drew's residence in September, Russell had borrowed a derringer pistol from him. Russell kept the pistol only about a week, before returning it to Sterling the day after he left Boise for Oneida.

The defense called Ben Drew next. He related to the jury that he had known Russell Morford for 17 years and Amanda 15, and that until September 8, Russell had always been friendly. He testified that Russell and his wife lived in Hart's Exchange until their separation when Russell asked Drew to let his wife stay there. Then Drew testified to the confrontation that took place at his house on September 8.

After Drew, the climactic witness took the stand, Theodore Burmester.[115] The defense began by having Theodore explain the events of November 7—from the time when he, surrounded by points and authorities in the case he was working on, Carlton versus Hawkins, to the point after the shooting when he walked into town and straight to Henry Prickett's office. When he arrived, he exclaimed, "Great God Prickett, what I was talking to you about last night has come to pass. Morford attacked me this morning and fired three shots at me, and I fired three shots at him, and my last shot struck him, and I may have killed him."

Theodore then explained the events of the evening before the shooting. He told the jury how he had run into Russell at Hart's Exchange as he went to pick up tickets to the St. Clair Lecture—the confrontation there in the bar with Russell—and the very near confrontation after the lecture and his retreat to Henry Prickett's office. There he asked Prickett to lend him a firearm which the latter agreed to do. Then Theodore testified he went to Joe Oldham's Saloon where he had a drink and then went home to bed.

A juror inquired of Theodore, "Did he give you the pistol?"

"No sir," Theodore testified in reply. "He said the pistol was at his home where he was boarding, and the folks had gone to

---

bed and he would get it to me the next morning. When I got the pistol, I stuck it in the waist of my pants."

From there Theodore moved on to how he and Russell Morford met. Then he gave his version of the infamous buggy rides with Amanda Morford.

Theodore's lawyers then asked him about the salacious testimony of A.J. Vincent. To which he indignantly replied, "I have heard the testimony of Vincent, and it is an infamous lie! There is not one word of truth in it. It is as false as God is true! It is false from beginning to end. It is an infamous lie! It is as false as God is true!"

Theodore was then asked to explain when and how he first learned that Amanda intended to divorce her husband. Theodore told the jury about the incident in Hart's Exchange when Russell first told him his suspicions about Colonel Preston and the subsequent announcement by Amanda. Although the divorce announcement testimony went uncontroverted throughout the trial, it was largely incapable of controversy, regardless of whether it was true or not because Theodore was the only person who testified to it since Morford was dead and Amanda did not testify.

Theodore then laid out the gory consequences of the ridiculously conflicted lawyer-client relationship he entered into when he agreed to represent his close friend's wife in their divorce. After Amanda moved into Ben Drew's home, Russell was despondent, living alone in his room in Hart's Exchange. In an effort to assist his friend, Theodore invited Russell to move in with him where they slept in the same bed in Theodore's office. One day during a break between client visits while still in this absurd cohabitant/opposing party relationship Russell asked to talk to Theodore privately. When they sat down, according to Theodore's testimony, Russell said to him, "I think Mrs. Morford will get over this in a little while and come back, particularly if I fight her a little. Won't you stand in with me and help me?"

Theodore upbraided Russell, sounding rather hypocritical, "No I cannot do that; you know that I have been engaged in your presence by her; and you know for me to take your side of the case would be unprofessional."

Theodore's lawyer then asked him about the scene at Ben Drew's house to which he gave his version of events. He also replied to questions about George Greathouse's assertion that he was in the bedroom alone with Amanda when Greathouse came over with the peaches. He did not deny any of the allegations though he said he did not remember being on the bed with Amanda when Greathouse came in. He explained however, that he was only grudgingly there because Russell had not returned from gambling and as a consequence Theodore missed out on a run with his friend (and by then the prosecutor) Major Foote. He further told the jury that not only did he tend to Amanda when she was sick, but he had spent several nights in the same room tending to Russell when he was ill.

Finally, on direct examination, Theodore provided a harmless explanation for the accusation that he had been with

Amanda at the races. Theodore explained that he had escorted a
Mrs. Miller to the races. However, at one-point George Coe left
Amanda with him and Mrs. Miller in Theodore's buggy until Coe
returned. Thirty minutes later Coe returned with an old
acquaintance of Amanda's named Lynch, and Amanda climbed
back into Coe's buggy and spent the rest of the day with Mr.
Lynch.

With that, the defense attorney relinquished control of the
witness to the prosecutor for cross examination, what the Supreme
Court has termed the single greatest legal engine for the discovery
of truth. Despite the revered position cross examination enjoys in
the pantheon of beloved American tools of justice, the cross
examiner shed no more light on Theodore's actions leading up to,
during, and immediately following the shooting than what he had
already given on direct examination. During the cross examination
there was only one emotional outburst, having more to do with
scandalous dirt than substance. Apparently not satisfied with
Theodore's explanation that after he had dropped off Mrs. Drew
following the St. Clair lecture, he was on Eighth Street on his way
to his office when he saw Russell Morford. The prosecutor
insisted that Theodore tell the jury where he had been immediately
before he saw Russell that night. The newspaper account implies
an outburst from Theodore followed by an attempted retraction:
"don't know that it was important where I was before that time;
was going up towards my office from Main Street; the reason why
it was not important where I had been is because I might have

been to a _____ [whore?] house. But did not say that I was; but had been down town [*sic*] to take a drink; that was the truth about it."

The cross examination ended by forcing Theodore to deny the most salacious portions of James Reynolds' assertions—that Theodore said he wanted to bring an end to the trouble by forcing a violent confrontation and that he said that he was no more guilty for shooting Russell than if he had "shot a dog in the street."

And so ended the testimony of the accused, but it was not quite the end of the case for the defense. The defense recalled Henry Prickett and once again attempted to elicit the substance of Theodore's conversation with Prickett the night before the shooting. However, Judge Noggle still would have none of it. The defense likely argued something like the rule of completeness— the People had first offered the statements Theodore had purportedly made about his conversation with Prickett to James Reynolds. Moreover, Theodore refuted making the statements. As a consequence, the defense was entitled to try to resolve the controverted assertion initiated by the People by having the person to whom the statements were originally made testify as to whether they were said. In that context they are not even hearsay because they are not offered for the truth of the matter, only that they were said at all. In any event the defense arguments fell on deaf ears and Prickett was not allowed to testify to the conversation.

The defense also called Amanda's physician, Dr. Partlow, who testified that much of her health problems derived from lack of sleep caused from staying up late at night waiting for her husband to return from gambling binges. The amazing part of this testimony is not the absurd pseudo scientific assertion the "doctor" made, but even if it were true, how it was relevant to anything. Amanda's physical ailments had no bearing on any secondary issue, much less the ultimate one—was Theodore justified in shooting Russell. At best it was an attempt to bootstrap evidence of Russell's bad character, that he was a gambler.

The final defense witness was Joseph Pinkham; instead of ending with a strong emotional witness (Theodore) the defense team had Pinkham tell the jury that Russell Morford's character was streaky. For a week or more at a time he would be diligent and hard working. But then he would descend into drinking and gambling binges, staying out until all hours of the night. Indeed, Amanda had left Russell the previous summer for the same reason—Russell's gambling—but she had quickly returned to him when he came to get her. In all dealings with her, Pinkham observed, Russell had always been courteous and giving to Amanda. So instead of ending with a refutation of the People's case as would have happened if the defense had ended with Theodore, the defense case ended with "Morford was always courteous in his dealings with Amanda." Suffice it to say, it was not a strong way to end.

The January 13, 1870 edition of the Idaho Tri-Weekly Statesman published the "Conclusion of Evidence," in the "Burmester Trial." Although the title asserts the witnesses gave

"Testimony For the Defense," it appears erroneous. The witnesses appear to be prosecution witnesses rebutting portions of the defense case. For example, Daniel Dwight was apparently rushed out to the Watkins home to see what he could of the shooting scene from that vantage point. He was also called upon to restate in more certain terms that it was Theodore who shot first. H.C. Riggs and Sam Clayton were also called to testify that they could see the scene clearly from the Watkins' and the "Mexican's" houses. Clayton and Ron Davis also testified how nicely Russell treated Amanda. Jonas Brown then testified that Amanda showed up at the funeral house where Russell's corpse lay and she broke down with grief, as if that shed any light on something even remotely of consequence to the case. John Hailey denied Russell had said some of the things that Theodore attributed to him during the confrontation at Ben Drew's home. Finally, Robert Irwin took the stand to refute Hultz's testimony about the tense nature of the meeting between Russell and Theodore at Hart's Exchange on November 6. Yet, in the end, he conceded in response to a juror's question, that he too heard Hultz ask Theodore, "What is the matter with Judge Morford?" More to the point he could not explain why Irwin would ask such a question if the meeting had not been emotionally charged.

The testimony likely ended late on Wednesday and the sides retired for the evening. I imagine the lawyers and the judge argued some points about the instructions Judge Noggle was to give the jury and then both parties went to their respective offices to prepare their final arguments.

That next morning the court was full of spectators although there were no women present due to "the inclemency of the weather."[116] Ned Holbrook gave the initial closing argument for the People with a speech that lasted an hour and a half. The defense split their work up between two of the lawyers from their team. John McBride spoke first for two hours before being relieved by the renowned orator, Frank Ganahl, who spoke for another three and a half hours! By the time he finished it was 7:00 p.m. Major Romily Foote then gave a "terse and logical" rebuttal that lasted a mere solitary hour.

By that time the jury had been subjected to eight hours of speeches. However, their torture had not yet ended for the judge had yet to instruct them on the law which took another hour and a quarter.

Neither the Idaho Tri-Weekly Statesman nor the Idaho World reported the content of the arguments of either party, though they went to great lengths to report each lawyer spoke eloquently. The Idaho World dedicated considerable space to praising the speech and abilities of Ganahl while not reporting a single word much less a summary of it. It is interesting to compare the style of this report to that of any modern report from a daily

---

[116] "The Burmester Trial," *Idaho World*, Dec. 30, 1869, 2.

paper reporting on a noteworthy trial. The Idaho World wrote about Ganahl:

> It is a difficult matter to give anything like a correct estimate of Mr. Ganahl's speech. It is almost sufficient to say that Frank Ganahl spoke. He not only fully sustained his well deserved reputation as an orator on this occasion, but even surpassed himself. His flow of language seemed inexhaustible; he threw his whole heart and soul into his cause, and held the Court, jury and audience spell-bound by such eloquence that it has never been our good fortune to listen to before. He was pleading the cause not only of his client but his friend, and he did justice to both. [117]

As a prosecutor today, my colleagues and I feel quite fortunate when a single quote from a closing argument finds its way into a newspaper article about an important case we have just summed up. A critique of the overall speech is a horrifying prospect to even consider. I'm not sure what would be worse, an orgy of acclaim like Ganahl received or a page full of derision.

After the lawyers made their cases the judge "charged the jury." The act of reading the instructions to the jury has to be the most tedious task of any jury trial. Both the Idaho World and the Tri-Weekly Statesman were displeased with Judge Noggle's performance. After the World heaped praise upon praise for Ganahl and his speech, it derided Noggle for taking the jury instructions home with him and "thus mutilating the records of the

---

[117] Ibid.

court," and making it impossible to publish the instructions, as if someone would voluntarily read them. But, the World confided, the paper's writers were able to learn "something of the nature of the charge given by this picayune edition of Jeffreys, or rather imbecile imitator of the bloody judge, and from what [they] learn[ed] the charge was in every way worthy of the man from whom it emanated."[118]

That was not the only criticism the Idaho World had for Judge Noggle. The Idaho World in its December 30, 1869 issue editorialized in its reportage on the trial that the judge had been performing adequately until the prosecution sought to bring up Theodore's "previous conduct...towards Mrs. Morford...." When the defense objected the Court overruled "and from that time forward opened the flood gates and admitted all the scandal and gossip which had been going the rounds of Boise City...." "Whether Judge Noggle erred through ignorance or design we are unable to say, but are satisfied that a prurient curiosity and desire to hear all of what he thought would prove a rehash of the dirty details of scandal and gossip, in which he had participated to some extent himself, had a great deal to do with his ruling on the admission of such testimony."[119] Thus the Idaho World believed that the judge was transparently partial toward the prosecution.

At the end of a very long day the case was finally submitted to the jury. In contrast to the attorneys, the jury wasted

---

[118] Ibid.
[119] Ibid.

no time and returned with their verdict in less than thirty minutes, finding the defendant, Theodore Burmester, not guilty of murder.

While the Idaho World spewed its vitriol at the Judge, the Idaho Tri-Weekly Statesman saved its bile for the jury. The Statesman claimed that the city received the news of the jury in disbelief for it was "impossible that such a verdict could be arrived at by an intelligent jury."[120]

The paper that had so recently cried out at the pain Theodore had suffered at the murder of his wife now scoffed at the plausibility of his defense. While the World thought that the evidence regarding the scandalous summer liaison between Theodore and Amanda had no more to do with the murder than the proceedings at the opening of the Suez Canal would have had,[121] the Statesman thought that evidence central. Indeed, the Statesman argued that the shooting had its genesis in the "summer evening tete and promenades."[122] Finally, the Statesman condemned the verdict, but consoled its readers by remarking that "Burmester is aquit [sic], but the effect upon society is all the same as though this terrible outrage upon public morals as well as human life had been punished as the law directs, and as its merits deserve."[123]

Vigilante Justice

James S. Reynolds, editor of the Idaho Tri-Weekly Statesman, was incensed by the jury's verdict in the Burmester

---

[120] "Burmester's Acquittal," *Tri-Weekly Statesman*, Dec. 28, 1969, 3.
[121] "The Burmester Trial," *Idaho World*, Dec. 30, 1969, 2.
[122] "Burmester's Acquittal," *Tri-Weekly Statesman*, Dec. 28, 1969, 3.
[123] Ibid.

case. Reynolds embodied the ideal of romanticism and as such he had very definite ideas concerning right, wrong, and justice. The Burmester verdict did not meet his expectation of justice. He warned his readers that another tribunal, the moral sense of the community, would judge him guilty even if the regularly impaneled jury did not.[124] Although this statement sounds like he was merely expressing his frustration and invoking karma, James Reynolds may have intended a different, subtler, message to specific members of the Boise community.

James S. Reynolds had been one of the three members of the executive committee of the Boise Vigilantes.[125] The executive committee possessed ultimate power to determine when the vigilantes would take action and order someone's death as well as when they would compel the marked person to leave town. Because the jury had failed to act as Reynolds and the executive committee believed justice demanded, the executive committee ordered Theodore's death by hanging.[126] Notice was sent to the general membership of the Boise Vigilantes so that they could assemble, arm themselves and get ready to take action.[127]

Somehow Amanda received word of the executive committee's decision and she immediately made her way to the assembly point. There she implored the committee to be merciful. Apparently, they had a weakness for the entreaties of concerned

---

[124] Ibid.
[125] Donaldson, *Idaho of Yesterday*, 168.
[126] Ibid., 163.
[127] Ibid., 162.

women. Later in 1870, the tearful beseeching of a wife of a marked man resulted in a death sentence being commuted to banishment and that is what happened in this case. Amanda convinced the committee to change their verdict and instead of death ordered that Theodore leave town—for good. It is not recorded who had the grim task of notifying Theodore that he had been banished nor whether, if ever, he knew how close he had come to a death sentence at the hands of the Vigilantes. After notification Theodore quietly moved back to Oregon to pick up the pieces of his shattered life with his two young boys.

Chapter 6: Starting Over

Theodore had always been impulsive and a bit tempestuous. But after the death of his beloved Ariminta, Theodore's behavior simply turned reckless. The loss left him adrift.

Fleeing Idaho, Theodore moved back to Oregon where he was reunited with his sons. Still just as lost, he was nevertheless forced to resume some semblance of a family life for the sake of Frank and William.

The loss must have been crushing. He immediately sought to fill that terrible void by finding someone to take Ariminta's place as mother to his young sons and in his own heart as well. Perhaps, subconsciously that is what he was trying to do with Amanda Morford. In any event, after moving to Oregon in January, he remarried six months later on June 8, 1870. This time he married a young woman from Linn County named Jemima Humphries. Dana, as she was called, bore him a daughter in 1872. Particularly revealing his sense of loss was the name he gave this child: Mildred Ariminta. However, any happiness he might have gleaned from the birth of this child was dashed when the following year young William, the baby John Konapeck had placed in the wagon as he prepared to incinerate Theodore and Minnie's house, died.

Following his younger son's death, Theodore moved his family that same year to Utah Territory. It appears that initially at least, Theodore moved to Bingham, a rapidly expanding mining camp on the western side of the Salt Lake Valley.

Bingham Canyon in the Oquirrh Mountains had only supported perhaps 100 miners until 1870. The completion of the transcontinental railroad made it a more economically sound proposition to remove ore from the Bingham mine for smelting elsewhere.[128] Consequently the camp attracted more activity. 276 persons reported that they lived in Bingham in the 1870 census. In "1871, Bingham was organized as a voting precinct of Salt Lake County" enabling the citizens there to participate in elections for county officers and elect their own constable.[129] One of the early constables in the rough and tumble town was none other than William Burmester, Theodore's brother.

In 1873, rail connections were completed linking Bingham to the outside world. By the following year the voting district claimed a population of 1400, with 800 of those living within Bingham City.[130]

Though probably not more violent than other mining camps, Bingham was peopled by a population that was by-in-large, single, young, male, and armed, a combination that tends toward violence still today. Importantly in that regard, it was serviced by six saloons.[131]

---

[128] Lynn R. Bailey, *Old Reliable: A History of Bingham Canyon, Utah*, (Tucson: Westernlore Press, 1988), 69.
[129] Ibid., 69-70.
[130] Ibid., 70.
[131] Ibid., 71.

Theodore had no connections to Utah in 1873 other than his brother. Thus, it seems likely that William's presence in Bingham City was the link that drew Theodore to Utah Territory. Having first secured the position as constable, William may have invited Theodore or possibly, Theodore searching for yet another new start after his young boy's death, chose his brother's town as a place to begin.

Theodore's impetuosity appears on the record soon after his arrival in Bingham. Theodore quarreled there with a man named McManus although the substance of their argument is no longer preserved.[132] During the course of the dispute passions flared even hotter until the parties drew guns on one another. Finally, Theodore had enough and fired his gun at McManus but missed. Instead he struck an innocent bystander named Mike Fagan.[133]

The sound of the gunshot in the small town drew the attention of the constable, Theodore's brother, William, who came running to the scene. Upon his arrival, William attempted to arrest McManus, who declined to be taken into custody peaceably. McManus resisted William's efforts and turned his firearm on the constable. McManus' aim was better than Theodore's but not by much. He struck William in the chest and the stomach but a third shot ricocheted and struck the hapless Fagan again.

---

[132] Ibid., 72. Bailey misspells Theodore's and William's name as "Burmiester."
[133] Ibid.

Bystanders finally wrestled control of the gun from McManus and placed him under arrest. Fagan was taken to "Clay's saloon to patch his body and restore his spirits."[134] McManus was subsequently convicted of disorderly conduct and resisting arrest.[135] Though he had been shot in the stomach and chest, William did not succumb to his wounds. He moved to Stevensville, Montana, where he worked mostly at mining.[136]

By 1874 Theodore was practicing law in Salt Lake City. He eventually entered into a long partnership with another attorney, Enos D. Hoge. About the time Theodore arrived in Utah, Hoge, as part of the defense team, was taking part in the great legal theater that was the prosecution of John D. Lee, the only person ever prosecuted for the Mountain Meadows Massacre.[137] Although he had an active practice in Salt Lake City, Theodore filed a homestead claim in Tooele County. This foundation in Tooele set roots for Frank from which he would subsequently blossom.

All the while it must have become more and more apparent that Theodore and Dana were ill-matched, and that Theodore had leaped into this relationship prematurely. This union was finally torn asunder on November 25, 1881. Dana and little

---

[134] Ibid., 72-73.

[135] Ibid., 73.

[136] Obituary, *Missoulian (MT)*, Aug. 31, 1883. The obituary also claims that William shot two men, each in self-defense after he himself had first been shot. Likely one of these shootings is the Bingham incident and perhaps that was how McManus was finally subdued, William had shot him.

[137] Will Bagley, *Blood of Prophets: Brigham Young and the Massacre at Mountain Meadows*, (Norman: University of Oklahoma Press, 2002), 291.

Mildred Ariminta moved back to Oregon leaving Theodore and Frank to fend for themselves. But, by this time Frank was nearly a grown man; approximately the age when Theodore had crossed the Isthmus of Panama.

Theodore would not remain alone for long, and after only a year he married for the third time. This time he married a woman from Grantsville in Tooele County, Utah named Maria Finch. Their first child was born on December 10, 1883, a daughter they named Minnie.

Over the next eight years Maria and Theodore had four more children. Following Minnie there was Henry, born in 1885 who became the newspaper editor. Then 2 years later came Wilma, short for Wilhelmina, named after her grandmother Wilhelmina Fredericka Josephina Heiner. Another two years passed and along came another daughter they called Theodora. All of these children were born in Grantsville despite Theodore's purchase of a residence at 134 East 300 South, in downtown Salt Lake City.[138] Maria and Theodore would have one more child, Marion Louise, born in 1891, but this time in Salt Lake City.

Theodore likely carried on old Boise friendships even after he moved to Utah Territory. In various reports, the Salt Lake Tribune noted the presence of S. P. Scaniker, Joseph Rosborough

---

[138] That house was located where a public building now stands, across the street from the office where I worked when writing this book.

and John R. McBride.[139] For McBride, moving to the Salt Lake Valley in the 1870s would actually best be described as a "return" because as a fourteen-year-old boy he traveled through Utah en route to Oregon.

The year was 1846 and the McBride family wagon train had stopped at Fort Bridger to rest and refit for the final push to Oregon. During their stay they met a famous trapper named Captain Walker, a charismatic man of "about fifty years of age, six feet in height and strongly built."[140] Through his travels as a trapper Walker had visited the Salt Lake Valley and thought it to be an ideal location for settlement. As luck would have it, Walker had known McBride's father decades before and immediately set about trying to convince the elder McBride and the other settlers to alter their destination from the Willamette to the Salt Lake Valley.

Initially, the men in the party were intrigued by Captain Walker's vivid descriptions of a valley with a "mild climate, a fertile soil, abundance of timber for all the purposes of settlement, and that it would necessarily become the center of the Indian and fur trade...for all the Rocky Mountain country."[141] Although the women in the party quickly vetoed the notion of settling in an

---

[139] E.g., "Successful Hunters," *Salt Lake Tribune*, Aug. 22, 1874. Rosborough and McBride returned to Salt Lake City from a hunting trip near Soda Springs. This strange little article then lists the game that they bagged including "bear, grouse, antelope, gees, turkeys, snipe, wild boars and hippopotami."

[140] John R. McBride, "Pioneer Days in the Mountains," *Tullidge's Quarterly Magazine*, vol. 3, no. 3, (July 1884), 317.

[141] Ibid., 318.

unknown wilderness, 1000 miles either direction from friends and loved ones, a few of the men formed a detachment to explore the Salt Lake Valley and validate for themselves Captain Walker's claims. Young McBride volunteered to go with the detachment and when he first laid eyes on the Great Salt Lake he was awestruck at the sight of a single place where sea met river, plain and mountain. The little party continued south past warm springs near where Bountiful is today. Finally, they entered the valley from the hill where the capital building now rises. From a perch near there, shaded by a copse of ancient cottonwoods with no underbrush, the band of explorers could see lines of trees emerge from Parley's, Millcreek, and both Cottonwood Canyons like long narrow forested fingers that traced the course of their streams emanating from the canyons. Despite its idyllic beauty, the detachment quickly turned around and rejoined their main party in the Snake River Valley.

Later that same year the Donner Party found the serenity of the empty valley too alluring to quickly move on after an arduous journey over the Rocky Mountains. Only when they had been there a week and awoke one morning to discover a thin crust of ice had formed on their water buckets did they realize they ought not terry any longer. They hurriedly packed and continued the trek west, but alas it was too late. After leaving the Salt Lake Valley the Donner Party was famously trapped in a severe blizzard in the Sierra Nevada Mountains. The following year, 1847, the

Mormons arrived and fulfilled Captain Walker's dream of a permanent settlement in the Salt Lake Valley.

In Utah Theodore made new friends as well. Of course, he met his third wife, Maria Finch, who was from Tooele County. In addition, he became an acquaintance of Joshua Reuben Clark Sr., father of the famous lawyer, statesman and leader in the Church of Jesus Christ of Latter-day Saints and for whom the Brigham Young University College of Law is named.

Clark Sr. and Theodore lived close enough to one another that they might have been considered neighbors in a community of farmers and ranchers.[142] There, they had several interactions, usually concerning court proceedings. On one occasion Clark Sr. was frustrated with Theodore and his client, Newton Dunyou. Apparently, Dunyou had pleaded with the plaintiffs, Kimball and Clark, asking for more time to hire an attorney. They relented but did not return the summons. So, when Theodore showed up for court he moved for a dismissal of the action, non-suit, because the plaintiffs had not returned the summons in the time that the statute required.[143]

Of all his friendships, both new and old, Theodore's closest and longest lasting friendship was with the famed Methodist Missionary, Thomas Corwin Iliff. According to Theodore's daughter, Wilma, so close was their friendship that

---

[142] Joshua Reuben Clark Sr., "Journal Transcriptions," L. Tom Perry Special Collections, Harold B. Lee Library, Brigham Young University (2005), July 15, 1881.

[143] Clark Sr., "Journal Transcriptions," Nov. 22, 1880.

they entered into a mutual promise that the first to die would be
eulogized by the survivor.

Thomas Cowin Iliff

Born in 1845, Thomas Corwin Iliff grew to be a stout
young fellow made all the more so from strenuous farm work on
his father's Ohio farm.[144] His parents were fervent abolitionists,
opening up their home as an underground railroad station house
for fleeing slaves. When war broke out between the states there
was little doubt on whose side the Iliff boys would fight. Thomas
and his older brother raced down to enlist but Thomas was crest
fallen when the recruiters rejected him because he was only fifteen
years old. His brother made it in and was subsequently wounded in
action. Two years later, still young and naïve regarding the horrors
of war, he was afraid the war might pass him by. As he was
plowing his father's field one bright spring day, he likely dwelled
on his brother's sacrifice and his fear the war might end before he
got his chance. Thomas suddenly threw down his plow right there
in the field and went straight to the recruiting station for the 88th
Ohio Volunteers.[145] Once again the recruiters demanded his age
because he had to be eighteen to enlist. This time however,
Thomas was prepared, and he told them he was "going on
nineteen."[146] The recruiters accepted his word and he enlisted as

---

[144] James David Gillilan, *Thomas Corwin Iliff, Apostle of the Home Missions in the Rocky Mountains*, (New York: The Methodist Book Concern, 1919), 21.
[145] Ibid.
[146] Orson F. Whitney, *History of Utah In Four Volumes, vol. IV Biographical*, (Salt Lake City: George Q. Cannon and Sons, 1904), 633.

an infantry private. He did not stay with the infantry long, however. He was subsequently allowed to reenlist in the 9th Ohio Volunteer Cavalry (OVC). Thomas served in the 9th OVC until the end of the war. During that time Thomas and the 9th would participate in 60 engagements against Confederate forces.[147]

According to Larry Stevens' compilations of actions involving the 9th OVC, the 9th fought initially in Kentucky and Tennessee.[148] They remained in Knoxville as a police force and later moved on to patrol the Tennessee River around Athens and Florence Alabama. By July of 1864, the 9th OVC joined General Sherman's main force in the siege of Atlanta.[149] In mid-July the 9th OVC was sent out as part of a raid beyond the infantry lines to disrupt Confederate supply operations over the Atlanta and West Point Railroad.[150] The command consisted of 2500 cavalry troopers of which 700 were from the 9th OVC. The raid took place over 12 grueling mid-July days in sweltering Georgia heat. Throughout the operation the men and horses were either on the march, tearing up railroad, or fighting 20 hours of every day. When they finally staggered back into Union lines on July 22nd the men and their horses were exhausted, but the commanders felt good about having destroyed twenty-five miles of important railroad track and the 9th OVC itself had lost only twenty-six men

---

[147] Gillilan, *Apostle of the Home Missions*, 22.

[148] http://www.ohiocivilwar.com/cwc9.html; See also Whitney, *History of Utah In Four Volumes*, 633.

[149] Whitelaw Reid, *Ohio in the War: Her Statesmen, her Generals, and Soldiers*, vol. 2, (New York: Moore Wilstach & Baldwin, 1868), 812.

[150] Reid, *Ohio in the War*, 811.

captured while foraging (unfortunately most of these men would later die in Andersonville prison).

Only two days later, the 9th OVC was ordered back out on an ill-fated raid led by General McCook. General Sherman received startling news on August 1 when a colonel from a Tennessee cavalry unit that had come in contact with McCook's Division out in the field reported that McCook's entire Division "had been overwhelmed, defeated, and captured at Newnan," Georgia by a superior Confederate force.[151] Nevertheless, the Union Commander still held out hope. The next day Sherman was rewarded when McCook returned and reported what had happened. After initial success on the raid near Lovejoy Station, the Division had been surrounded by a larger Confederate force, and the Federal cavalrymen had been forced to fight their way out of the encirclement. McCook lost 600 men killed and captured in the break out.[152] Fortunately, for the 9th OVC the men and horses had been so exhausted by the earlier raid that very early in the operation McCook had been forced to leave them behind to guard a pontoon bridge at the Chattahoochee River. After repelling a Confederate attack there, the 9th OVC returned to Union lines twenty-four hours later.[153]

Iliff and the 9th OVC remained with Sherman for the rest of the war, participating in the March to the Sea following the

---

[151] William Tecumseh Sherman, *Memoirs of William T. Sherman*, New York: Literary classics of the United States, Inc., 1990), 570.
[152] Ibid. 571.
[153] Reid, *Ohio in the War*, 812.

capture of Atlanta, and fighting in one of the last skirmishes of the war in the Carolinas.[154] Iliff "witnessed" General Johnston's surrender to Sherman that effectively terminated organized resistance to the Union.[155]

Following the war, Iliff was mustered out of the army and he entered Ohio University. He studied at a furious pace, completing his six-year degree in five.[156] He was ordained a pastor in the Methodist Church and assigned the Coolville Circuit, riding from town to town ministering to townsfolk along the way. After only a few months however, he was made Missionary to the Rocky Mountains, a large district encompassing some of the most difficult mission fields in the world. Included in the territory was Bozeman, Montana where he first lived along with about 100 other white Americans in the midst of the Nez Perce tribe. The Rocky Mountain Mission area also included Utah Territory where a few Protestants and Catholics lived surrounded by a sea of Latter-day Saints.

Before he left though, he proposed to his love, Mary A. Robinson, and on March 22, 1871 the young couple wed. Robinson was a cousin to a man who would, like her husband, become an important national leader in the Methodist Church,

---

[154] W. D. Hamilton, "In at the Death, or the Last Shot at the Confederacy," in *Sketches of War History 1861-1865; Papers Prepared for the Commander of the State of Ohio Military Order of the Loyal Legion of the United States, vol. 6*, eds. Brevet Col. Theodore F. Allen et al., Wilmington (N.C.): Broadfoot Publishing Co., , 1908), 287-89.

[155] Whitney, *History of Utah In Four Volumes*, 633.

[156] Gillilan, *Apostle of the Home Missions*, 22.

Charles Cardwell McCabe. After the wedding the young couple set off for the wild country of Montana.

By 1873 Thomas and Mary were living in Bozeman. Every summer, the Nez Perce men left the Bozeman camp and rode to "the Yellowstone country" to hunt buffalo.[157] By the time Thomas and Mary arrived, the Yellowstone was occupied by the Sioux who resented other tribes hunting in what they regarded as their territory. Thus, the trip was frequently fraught with violence and hence only the men made the trip.

Mary was still new to the west and knew very little about the indigenous people. Indeed, all she knew about them was what she had gleaned from salacious books written for eastern city dwellers' consumption that reduced Native Americans to one-dimensional blood-thirsty savages.

One day, as the Nez Perce men prepared to depart for the summer hunt, "Amos, chief 'medicine man' for the tribe" marched into Mary's home and on into her kitchen without any warning or permission.[158] According to Mary, "the Indian never stops to knock at a door."[159] Thomas was not home at that moment and so Mary was all alone. Given her lack of any real understanding of indigenous people she lived in "abject fear" of them and consequently surrendered to their least demand. On this occasion Amos carried "four or five dozen eggs" and demanded she boil

---

[157] Ibid., 52.
[158] Ibid.
[159] Ibid.

them for him. She complied with his request, even going so far as to act as though she was pleased to do his bidding. She was so consumed by ignorant fear that she would have complied with nearly any menial demand just to get him out the door.[160]

Later that year in the fall when the men returned from the hunt, Amos went directly to the Iliff home. Mary later described what happened next. "With great appearance of honest pride he thrust his hand into an old dirty gunny-sack he had and brought out six Sioux scalps, exclaiming: 'ugh, heap big present! Kill Sioux, take scalp! Present!'...Of course I could not do otherwise than express my delight(!) and thanks."[161]

Mary Robinson Iliff later explained that she came to understand that although to her at the time, Amos' gift seemed ghastly, it had been to him a sacrifice of great value. He had eagerly presented her this gift in response to her trifling act of boiling a few eggs. According to Mary Iliff, the social status of the Nez Perce male was greatly affected by the number of enemy scalps he possessed. This grim token was more valuable than money, gold or even useful things like buffalo robes or ponies.[162]

By 1876 Thomas Iliff was made presiding elder of Utah Territory and so he moved his family to Salt Lake City. There, he traveled across the state preaching at mining camps and other

---

[160] Ibid., 53.
[161] Ibid. (quoting Mary Robinson Iliff).
[162] Ibid., 53-54.

small communities.[163] Perhaps it was at this time that he met Theodore during a trip to Bingham or Tooele. However, he left Utah in 1881 and spent the better part of the next two years traveling across Europe—England and the Continent—and the Holy Lands—from Turkey to Egypt.

He returned to Utah following his travels and was made Superintendent of the Utah Mission. It was likely about this time Iliff and Theodore became close. As part of his duties Iliff assumed the helm of the First United Methodist Church that had been built in 1875.[164] That church was located just a block west of Theodore's house on 300 South. When Iliff became pastor of the congregation, it was still deeply in debt from the construction costs of the church building. So overmastering was the debt, that collapse of the congregation was a serious concern of the pastor.[165]

---

[163] Ibid., 138.

[164] *First United Methodist Church, 130 Years*, (Salt Lake City: First United Methodist Church, 2000), 4-5.

[165] The precise figure for the debt varies with the source. Gillilan places the amount of debt retired by McCabe's fund raising at $25,000 (a value of almost $500,000 today). Gillilan, *Apostle of the Home Missions*, 55. The First United Methodist Church claims McCabe raised two-thirds of the $75,000 total debt. *First United Methodist Church, 130 Years*, 4.

Young Thomas Corwin Iliff, by permission Margaret E. Schreve Archives, Iliff School of Theology.

First United Methodist Church, 300 South between West Temple and Main Street. Used by permission, Utah State Historical Society.

Chaplain McCabe, Mary Iliff's cousin, came to the rescue. He began a fund-raising campaign tour around the country to pay down the debt. He took with him Mary's gift from Amos the Nez Perce medicine man. Holding the nasty dried-out scalps aloft he regaled audiences with the story of how they came into this cousin's possession.[166] McCabe's stories about the Wild West with Native Americans and Latter-day Saints were popular with eastern crowds and very soon he was able to raise enough money to retire the church's debt.

Due to the vast distances between communities within the Rocky Mountain mission and from the church's home base back east, Iliff frequently traveled by rail. During one such trip a fellow traveler, whether emboldened by drink or fantasy loudly proclaimed that the South would rise again, and that he was eager to join in the fight. The boor continued to harass his neighbors with his obnoxious bragging. Thomas finally had enough when the lout asserted that he would gladly take up arms to fight the Civil War a second time.[167] Provoked into action by the braggart, Iliff stood up from his seat and walked up to the would-be confederate and said in a voice straight from a Sunday sermon in church:

> "'Excuse me, sir, you appear the essence of bravery and patriotism. I wish to ask you if you were in the late war of which you speak so eloquently.'
> 'No, I was not,' retorted the bully.

---

[166] Gillilan, *Apostle of the Home Missions*, 54-55.
[167] Ibid., 156.

'Well, I was,' said the peacemaking doctor, 'and it took all the fight out of me.'
The crowd roared and the crestfallen hero (never-to-be) retired to the smoker."[168]

Iliff spent most of two decades, the 1870's and 1880's in Utah. There he not only led his flock at First United Methodist, but he was active in political issues in Utah. Despite his many years in active service to the community in Salt Lake City, Iliff later publicly declared that, "Utah may well be regarded as the most difficult mission field on the entire globe...."[169] What made Utah such a difficult mission field was the absolute dominance of the Church of Jesus Christ of Latter-day Saints in all aspects of their lives for the vast majority of people living in the Territory.

---

[168] Ibid., 157.
[169] *First United Methodist Church, 130 Years,* 5.

Chapter 7: A Gentile in the Land of Zion

The Church of Jesus Christ of Latter-day Saints was founded by Joseph Smith in 1830.[170] In 1820, fourteen-year-old Smith and his family lived in a small cabin in Palmyra, New York.[171] To gain privacy he left the cabin for a clearing in the woods to pray. There he experienced the "first vision." Preceded by a pillar of light, God and Jesus Christ appeared to him extending a message of redemption and personal forgiveness of his own sins.[172] Subsequent visions introduced Joseph Smith to an angel called Moroni. Moroni informed Smith of the location of long-lost gold plates and two stones called the Urim and Thummim, by which he could translate the language engraved on the plates. However, when Smith tried to unearth the plates he was prevented from doing so by supernatural forces until around 1827 when he was spiritually mature.[173] Once he was granted permission to acquire the plates, Smith used the Urim and Thummim to translate the arcane language inscribed in the plates.[174] A friend and early convert to what later became known as the Church of Jesus Christ of Latter-day Saints, Martin Harris, was so eager to see the plates and know their content that he

---

[170] Richard Lyman Bushman, *Joseph Smith: Rough Stone Rolling*, (New York: Alfred A. Knopf, 2005), 35. Some might be more familiar with the now disfavored name: the "Mormons."

[171] Ibid., 39.

[172] Ibid., 39-40.

[173] Ibid., 45.

[174] Robert Newton Baskin, *Reminiscences of Early Utah*, (Salt Lake City: Baskin, 1914), 156; Bushman, *Joseph Smith*, 66.

assumed the duty of writing down Joseph's dictation from Joseph's wife, Emma. Joseph Smith and Harris worked together in a single room divided by a blanket hung over a rope, Smith on one side studied the plates with the aid of the stones which revealed the mysteries of the plates. Smith then orally translated the text into King James English while Harris who sat on the other side wrote it all down.[175] Though Harris was allowed to lift the covered plates he was forbidden from looking at them under the penalty of the wrath of God.[176] The plates, once translated, revealed what is now known as the Book of Mormon. It purported to be largely the work of a leader of a group of descendants of Jews who fled the Old World for the New World.[177]

Through this revelation, Smith claimed to restore the Church of Jesus Christ to its original state before centuries of Catholic and Protestant malfeasance and misfeasance had corrupted it.[178] The actual name he gave the church in 1830 was the Church of Christ.[179] Eight years later following further revelation, Smith changed the name of the church to the Church of Jesus Christ of Latter-day Saints.[180]

Smith's new religion espoused several dramatic departures from Protestant and Catholic doctrine that led to tension and even

---

[175] Fawn M. Brodie, *No Man Knows My History: The Life of Joseph Smith the Mormon Prophet*, 2nd ed., (New York: Vintage Books, 1995), 53.

[176] Ibid.

[177] Bushman, *Joseph Smith*, 85-86.

[178] See James E. Talmage, *Articles of Faith, Classics in Mormon Literature Edition*, (Salt Lake City: Deseret Book Co., 1981), 201-02.

[179] Bushman, *Joseph Smith*, 109.

[180] Ibid., 349.

hostility between his followers and others in the community. The Church of Jesus Christ of Latter-day Saints rejected the doctrine of the trinity, they canonized extra-biblical scripture beyond the bible, and espoused a belief in a spiritual existence prior to birth. However, no Latter-day Saint doctrine aroused the ire of nonbelievers as universally as the doctrine of plural marriage.

Plural marriage was not part of the original doctrine espoused in the Book of Mormon. Indeed, in several places in the Book of Mormon God seems to forbid the practice. For example, the Book of Jacob chapter 2 verse 27 states, "Wherefore, my brethren, hear me, and hearken to the word of the Lord: For there shall not any man among you have save it be one wife; and concubines he shall have none." But in 1843 Smith received a revelation apparently justifying polygamy; "David also received many wives and concubines, as also Solomon and Moses, my servants, as also many of my servants from the beginning of Creation until this time, and in nothing did they sin, save in those things which they received not from me. David's wives and concubines were given unto him by me by the hand of Nathan, my servant, and others of the prophets who had the keys of power, and in none of these things did he sin again against me, save in the case of Uriah and his wife."[181]

Conflict between Latter-day Saints and nonbelievers escalated. Angry locals forced the fledgling Church to flee each

---

[181] Baskin, *Reminiscences of Early Utah*, 157.

place they settled; first New York, Ohio, and then Missouri. In 1839 they established a new settlement they called Nauvoo in Illinois. However, anger and disagreement once again found the Church, as Smith was charged criminally for shutting down the publication of the Nauvoo Expositor and ordering the destruction of its printing press. In June 1844, while in jail in Carthage, Missouri awaiting trial, an angry mob attacked the jail. Joseph Smith and several other Church members were gunned down.[182] Once again, the movement was under siege and eventually compelled to flee. Their new leader, Brigham Young, led the "Saints" west to a new promised "Zion." As they entered the Salt Lake Valley in 1847, one year after John R. McBride's brief visit there, Brigham Young is supposed to have said, "This is the place," and that was where the main body settled. To this day, businesses and government throughout the state shut down on July 24 to celebrate—in a far grander fashion than July 4—the "Days of '47."

By the 1880's the territory was populated throughout by small predominantly Latter-day Saint settlements. In the Salt Lake Valley Latter-day Saints were well in the majority, however, much government power lay in the hands of federally appointed territorial officials who were among the minority of "gentiles."[183]

---

[182] Bushman, *Joseph Smith*, 539-50.

[183] Although there are several explanations for the use of this term by believers in the Church of Jesus Christ of Latter-day Saints, a common use is that the term "Gentile" means someone who is not a believer and thus outside the group of chosen people.

Because of their earlier experiences, the Church of Jesus Christ of Latter-day Saints identified with the Biblical story of Exodus. This "Zion," that would eventually be called Utah Territory was their refuge, their "promised land."

As for the nonbelievers, although polygamy was universally frowned upon, it was for some, not the only or even the least of their objections to the Church of Jesus Christ of Latter-day Saints. Theodore was not a member of the Church and of course had many friends who were "gentiles" as well. Of these friends, some were outspoken critics of the Church of Jesus Christ of Latter-day Saints. Whether their objection was polygamy or something else, the occasion for their public expression of criticism toward the Church arose whenever a proposal for Utah statehood was submitted to congress.

Thomas C. Iliff unsurprisingly was stridently opposed to Church of Jesus Christ of Latter-day Saints. His opposition to the Church was based on differences in theology as well as the practice of polygamy.

Throughout his tenure in Salt Lake City and after, Thomas C. Iliff spoke out against Latter-day Saint Theology and polygamy which he, like most Americans, equated as one. Notwithstanding his opposition to the Church he did not dislike its adherents; indeed, he claimed to count many of them among his friends.[184] Nevertheless, he acted on his opinion concerning the church

---

[184] Whitney, *History of Utah in Four Volumes*, vol. 4, 634.

throughout his life. Even after statehood he joined other protestant leaders from Salt Lake to protest the seating of a polygamist representative to Congress, Brigham H. Roberts.[185] He prepared a lecture that he then took on a speaking tour across the country which became quite popular. The lecture, entitled "Mormonism a Menace to the Nation,"[186] made clear that his dispute was with the hierarchy of the Church of Jesus Christ of Latter-day Saints, the institution itself, and its doctrine, and not the masses of the Latter-day Saints themselves. They, he claimed, were on the whole, "peaceable, industrious, temperate, and to the extent of their knowledge and freedom, well-meaning citizens."[187]

Iliff, and others, believed the Church of Jesus Christ of Latter-day Saints was a threat to national security. Although this was not a term in use at the time, it captures in modern terms their concerns accurately enough. In their view, no protestant religion in America was as centrally controlled as the Latter-day Saints. With one Prophet, Seer and Revelator at the helm, one man who acted as the "mouthpiece of God "like" Moses of old," this "restored gospel of Jesus Christ"[188] sounded to them a lot like Catholicism, another religion also mistrusted in largely protestant America at the time. This notion of perfect adherence to the orders of one man, not elected, clashed severely with the ideals of the reformation and purposes of the separation of the church and state

---

[185] Gillilan, *Apostle of the Home Missions*, 88-89.
[186] Ibid., 73-74.
[187] Ibid.
[188] Doctrine and Covenants 28:2 and 107:65-67; Talmage, *Articles of Faith*, 210.

written into the constitution. Iliff held that there were "four corner stones" to American liberty:

> [1]The idea of God and his revelation to man;
> [2]The true spirit of patriotism—'One country and one flag'; Separation of church and state;
> [3]The true American school, and no interference by priest, prophet, or pope;
> [4]The true idea of the home—one wife, and only one at a time, and she the crowned queen of that household.[189]

In his speech Iliff asserted that polygamy continued to be "believed, taught, and practiced" throughout Utah long after the Woodruff manifesto (God's revelation to the Mormon President Woodruff to end the practice in 1890).[190] He relied on this assertion as proof that Mormonism flew in the face of the last three corner stones. First, the Church of Jesus Christ of Latter-day Saints and its president, prophet, seer, and revelator commanded allegiance among the believers to a degree far greater than did the government of the United States. U.S. law forbade the practice of polygamy. The federal government wrested a concession from the Church—a renunciation of the practice in the Woodruff manifesto. Nevertheless, polygamy according to Iliff, continued to be taught, believed, and practiced by Mormons in wards and homes throughout Utah and the surrounding states. Thus, in Utah there was no separation of church and state, for in Utah the Church of

---

[189] Gillilan, *Apostle of the Home Missions*, 74.
[190] Ibid., 93; Jeffrey Nichols, *Prostitution, Polygamy, and Power: Salt Lake City, 1847-1918*, (Urbana: University of Illinois Press, 2002), 36.

Jesus Christ of Latter-day Saints was the state. Moreover, the practice continued to be taught to another generation by the prophet through a host of priests. Accordingly, the true American school did not exist in Utah. Of course, the continued practice of polygamy violated the fourth corner stone on its face according to Iliff.

In his 1911 lecture Iliff did not elaborate how the doctrines and teachings of the Church, other than polygamy, were a corruption of God's revelation to man. Perhaps the differences were well known. The target audience for the lectures was primarily protestant women. The purpose of the lecture was to inflame the housewives across the country and encourage them to bring pressure to bear on their husbands, so that they in turn would take political action against the "serpent," thus the focus of the lecture on polygamy. As ammunition beyond the presumption in his argument that the Church of Jesus Christ of Latter-day Saints violated his first corner stone, Iliff gave a brief history of Joseph Smith and his founding of the Church, casting Smith as a charlatan in order to buttress his claim that Church beliefs corrupted the first corner stone.

John R. McBride also spoke against the Church of Jesus Christ of Latter-day Saints. McBride testified before Congress on June 14, 1889 against Utah statehood (the territory's fifth attempt). McBride was well respected not only in the west but also in Washington. By this time McBride had been a congressman and a federal judge. Moreover, he had lived in the territory for the previous 15 or 16 years.

In his testimony he was unabashedly against statehood. However, he was not against statehood simply due to polygamy that was still practiced there by many Latter-day Saints. Polygamy according to McBride, was immoral but not the problem. Rather, to him, polygamy was merely a symptom of what he perceived as a greater evil of the Church of Jesus Christ of Latter-day Saints. In his opinion faithful adherence to the Church was not compatible with faithful citizenship. McBride testified that the citizens of Utah are "mere soldiers in an ecclesiastical army." "They do as they are told. Whenever they go to the polls and vote, they go, and they know what they are expected to do when they get there." At the time, Church leadership attempted to distinguish "celestial" plural marriage and bigamy. McBride argued that though the proposed state constitution prohibited polygamy, the saints would continue to practice what they were told to do by the church leaders. Thus, the vast majority of the Utah residents would place their theocratic government at treasonous odds with the government of the United States. When the committee urged him to testify concerning Mormon Theology in comparison to others, he refused. His only concern was his belief that faithful Latter-day Saints were automatons whose allegiance ran only to the Church and not the nation.

The Liberal Party

In addition to complaints about alleged Latter-day Saint untrustworthiness, Church theology, and polygamy, other local gentiles complained about Latter-day Saint exclusive business practices.[191] The gentiles argued that in addition to political oppression, Latter-day Saints refused to patronize gentile businesses, while church businesses frequently operated as sanctioned monopolies.[192] Gentiles further claimed that higher taxes were assessed against them.[193] However, politically, there was little they could do about it locally since adherents to the Church of Jesus Christ of Latter-day Saints vastly outnumbered gentiles in the territory. Thus, men like McBride and Iliff who had national voices discouraged statehood. They preferred that federal appointees remain in place as a check against local elected leaders who would inevitably be Latter-day Saints.

The Liberal Party had its genesis in a group of gentile businessmen who regularly met in one of their offices to discuss the issues of the day.[194] During one such meeting in 1867 Robert Baskin suggested that one of their own, William McGoarty, run for Territorial delegate to Congress. The others agreed and McGoarty accepted the informal nomination. He received 105 votes. However, by the next election the group formally organized into the Liberal Party and met in convention in Corrine.[195]

---

[191] Nichols, *Prostitution*, 15; see also Baskin, *Reminiscences of Early Utah*, 24.

[192] Baskin, Reminiscences *of Early Utah*, 26.

[193] Nichols, *Prostitution*, 15.

[194] Baskin, *Reminiscences of Early Utah*, 23.

[195] A town north of Ogden and west of Brigham City.

In the years between the Civil War and the end of the century the Liberal Party in Utah Territory grew to express the views of the disenfranchised gentiles and excommunicated Latter-day Saint businessmen known as "Godbeites" who had dared oppose Brigham Young's plan for a Latter-day Saint protectionist economy.[196] By 1890 the party was able to actually win the Salt Lake City Mayoral election.[197] However, this had as much to do with influx of gentiles and the disenfranchisement of polygamous Latter-day Saints who had been imprisoned as it did to any clever political maneuvering. Indeed, the Party was extremely antagonistic toward their Latter-day Saint brothers in the county. Both Theodore and Thomas Iliff were in the thick of the fight on the side of the Liberal Party. Iliff and Burmester as well as Burmester's law partner, Enos D. Hoge were delegates to the Salt Lake County Liberal Party convention July 14, 1891 in Salt Lake City when they adopted an anti-statehood platform.[198]

During the convention Mr. Charles S. Varian read the party platform to the assembled body of the convention:

> The American citizens of Salt Lake county in Liberal convention assembled hereby present to their fellow-citizens their platform of principles.
> Whereas, For forty years the institutions of the free government of the United States have

[196] Nichols, *Prostitution*, 15.
[197] Ibid., 98.
[198] "The 'Liberal' Convention," *The Deseret Weekly*, 43, no. 5 (July 25, 1891): 148 (first precinct, first ward, Iliff; fourth precinct, eighteenth ward, E. D. Hoge; fifth precinct, eleventh ward, Theodore Burmester).

been menaced in this portion of American
territory by a theocracy so despotic in its exercise
of power to suppress all freedom of thought or
action in the individual; and

Whereas, During all of said time the
people acknowledging its authority have been
directed and educated in lines of thought tending
to induce the conviction that the government of
the United States was a league with death and a
covenant with hell and an enemy to them and their
institutions; and

Whereas, In the past the subordination of
temporal government to ecclesiastical power in
the Territory of Utah has made life unendurable,
and the pursuit of liberty and happiness
impossible for all true Americans within its
sovereignty; and

Whereas, The Liberal party, born
necessities of the hour, and made possible by the
union of brave and true men and women, by its
strong and steady opposition for these many years
past to the insolent demands of an arrogant and
alien priesthood has touched the pulse and
quickened the conscience of the people of these
United States; and

Whereas, The political conditions of the
one hundred and fifty thousand people produced
by years of mental slavery and superstition in the
natural order of things cannot possibly be changed
in a day; and

Whereas, All revelations, judging from
the lessons of history, come from within and not
from without; and

Whereas, The political power of the
Mormon Church in the Territory of Utah as
exercised in the past and as it now exists in the
present is a menace to free institutions too
dangerous to be suffered; now, therefore, be it

> Resolved, By the Liberal party of Salt Lake county in convention assembled that we announce to our fellow citizens of the United States that there is no question of a national political character which at the present time can serve to distract the attention of them and ourselves from the single one which here confronts us...

> Resolved, That the men and women who were educated under and believe in the principles of free government are not prepared to say to the people of the United States, at this time, that the Territory should become a State. When the people here shall have become emancipated, shall have renounced all dependence in secular matters upon a hierarchy; when they evidence by their own honest endeavors in a bona fide struggle for freedom that the spirit which leavens the institutions of the country prevails with them; when, in fact, there shall be no question that proper conditions exist—when that time comes, and not till then—are we willing that Utah shall become a free and sovereign State; because every interest of Utah, both Mormon and Gentile, forbids the admission of this Territory to statehood, under present conditions inasmuch as it would destroy values, demoralize business, and stretch around a polygamous theocracy the protection of State lines....[199]

As one might imagine, officials in the Church of Jesus Christ of Latter-day Saints did not appreciate the Liberal Party platform. Consequently, The Deseret Weekly, official organ of the Church of Jesus Christ of Latter-day Saints, published a critical

---

[199] "The "Liberal' Convention," *The Deseret Weekly*, 149.

response to the Liberal Party platform in the same issue in which
the weekly carried the platform. The article focused on Thomas
Iliff and argued that the Liberal Party platform was hypocritical in
its criticism of local Latter-day Saint government.

> AMONG the resolutions adopted unanimously, by
> a rising vote, three cheers and a tiger, at the
> "Liberal" convention July 14th, was this:
> "All revelations, judging from the lessons of
> history, come from within and not from without."
> Among the delegates who took active part in this
> convention was Rev. Dr. Iliff who has been quite
> energetic in his support of "Liberalism" in
> opposition to Republican and Democratic
> organization in Utah. This Gentleman is the
> leading Elder of the Methodist church in Utah and
> is much opposed to "Mormon" influence in
> politics. He thinks the Church and the state should
> be entirely separate; at least so he says. But what
> he objects to in a "Mormon" Elder he appears to
> think quite proper for a Methodist Elder.
>
> But that is a small matter compared with
> others that are brought to front. Yet we draw
> attention to the fact that "Liberalism" has once
> more demonstrated that it is an assault upon a
> religion, aye more, it is an assault upon Religion
> for all religions founded upon the idea that
> "revelations have come from without," that is
> from the Supreme Being to mortals. If Methodist
> creed is not built upon that foundation, then its
> whole history is a living lie.
>
> Methodism teaches that the Bible is the
> word of God, that God appeared and revealed
> Himself to Abraham, that He showed Himself to
> Moses and gave to him His law, including the ten
> commandments written on tables of stone by the
> finger of God; that He spake in times past by the

prophets and also by His Son Christ, as well as by angels sent from the courts of glory. These divine revelations were not "from within" but "from without." If they are not true, the Bible is a collection of fables, a mass of deception and fraud like "Liberalism" that Dr. Iliff has so lovingly espoused.

Christianity, in whatever form it appears today, was originally started on the doctrine of "revelation from without." The doctrine was not of mere internal impressions evolved from the mind of man, but of visitations from divine and angelic beings, and inspirations that come from the Holy Ghost sent down from heaven.

So with all the great religions of the world Manifestations and communications from the higher spheres to lower, not spontaneous imaginings and conceits were the sources from which they emanated.

The lessons of history teach the very reverse of the "Liberal" resolution. The Bible and all the sacred books of the ages and the nations are against it. The Methodist creed is emphatically at war with it. Dr. Iliff is in strange fellowship, endorsing as thoroughly infidel a resolution as was ever adopted by a convention of atheists.

Judge Zane in his address at the Republican convention said: "The People's party and the Liberal party have been organized with respect to religion. It is a bad thing to have political parties in any country organized with respect to religious faith and worship." For this he was savagely attacked by the "Liberal" organ, which with its accustomed brazen mendacity avowed that the "Liberal" party was not organized with respect to religion. The resolution we have quoted proves that Judge Zane's reference to the "Liberal" faction was correct. It is "organized with respect to religion." It is organized with respect to religious faith and worship. The resolution is not only against "Mormon" religious faith but against the religious faith and worship of all Christendom. And Rev. Dr. Iliff was one of the cheering crowd that adopted and endorsed the opposition.

Whatever reference to religion there may have been in the organization of the People's party it is certain that it never in any way dragged religious faith into its political conventions. That was left for the "Liberal" faction which is so emphatic against religion in politics.

We might have expected that the crowd which follows the gang at the head of the "Liberal" faction, and which includes all the most disreputable elements of the city, would echo the atheistical sentiment expressed in the resolution on revelation. But that the leading Methodist divine in Utah should join with them, is indeed surprising and provocative of great disgust "from within."[200]

Where was Theodore within this debate? He was a leader in the same party as Iliff and his law partner Hoge. The party's platform was stridently "anti-Mormon" as were Iliff's public statements. I think it not a great leap of logic to suspect that Theodore felt the same way. Nevertheless, as a defense attorney his professional duty was challenged by his personal beliefs when he came to represent a former police officer and well-connected Latter-day Saint named Brigham Young Hampton.

---

[200] "'Liberalism' and Religion," *The Deseret Weekly*, 43, no. 5 (July 25, 1891): 136-37.

Chapter 8: Defending Brigham Young Hampton

As his name might suggest, Brigham Young Hampton was a prominent member of the Church of Jesus Christ of Latter-day Saints.[201] Prior to 1885, Hampton had been a police officer in Salt Lake City. But, by 1885 he was the collector of licenses for Salt Lake City. Relations between Latter-day Saints and non-Mormons reached a new low after 1884 because the federal authorities had stepped-up prosecution for the practice of polygamy. Like most of his fellow Latter-day Saints, Hampton was extremely distraught over the subject.

Tensions between the Latter-day Saints and the gentiles in the territory first escalated with the Edmunds Act, making it a misdemeanor for a man to cohabit with more than one woman.[202] In addition, the Utah Commission required voters to swear an oath that they did not "cohabit with more than one woman" and added language not contained in the Edmunds Act: "in the marriage relation."[203] However, the government was still unable to effectively prosecute bigamy.

Several things changed all of that in 1884. First, Charles S. Zane arrived and assumed the posts of presiding judge of the Third Judicial District as well as Chief Justice of the Territorial Supreme Court.[204] Zane was not anti-Church in his outlook but insisted on strict compliance with the laws of the land. The second

---

[201] *People v. Hampton*, 4 Utah 259, 260 (1886).
[202] Nichols, *Prostitution*, 31.
[203] Ibid.
[204] Ibid., 32.

change came in the office of the United States District Attorney
when they began to vigorously prosecute for cohabitation rather
than plural marriage, and at the same time actively sought the
disqualification of any potential "grand juror who claimed to
believe in plural marriage." Thus, the polygamy prosecutions were
unimpeded by juries that might have contained any sympathetic
Latter-day Saints.

Soon, hundreds of Latter-day Saint men were convicted
and imprisoned and Church President John Taylor, and George Q.
Cannon went into hiding to avoid that same fate.[205] The Church of
Jesus Christ of Latter-day Saints complained to the President of
the United States that their religious freedom was being singled
out for attack. They tried to demonstrate to the President that the
policies carried out in the territory smacked of hypocrisy when the
Latter-day Saint men were being punished for engaging in
permanent marriage relationships while "[t]he paramour of
mistresses and harlots, secure from prosecution, walks the streets
in open day."[206]

In September 1885, undoubtedly a Latter-day Saint or
group of Latter-day Saints, angry with the polygamy prosecutions
filled several jars with human excrement and threw them through
the windows of the dwellings of the United States Attorney,
William H. Dickson, his law partner and Assistant United States

---

[205] Ibid.
[206] Ibid. (quoting Declaration of Grievances and Protests).

Attorney, Charles S. Varian, and United States Commissioner McKay.[207]

Brigham Young Hampton decided on an even more radical plan than "poop" bombs. He and his confederates concluded that if they could catch some of the Gentile leadership in the territory visiting prostitutes, it would clearly reveal the hypocrisy in the policy of the polygamy prosecutions. Moreover, they would suddenly have the leverage they needed to bring the hated policy to an end if they were to indict important enough gentile leaders. However, the plan quickly went awry. Hampton paid a couple of prostitutes to report on their customers, and soon thereafter he and his police officer confederates brought up a marshal on charges.[208] The United States Attorneys quickly caught on to the scheme and before long Charles Varien convened a Grand Jury to indict Hampton for conspiracy to operate a house of prostitution.

The trial began Dec 22, 1885. Due to the tremendous public interest in the case, the court room overflowed with spectators. Mayor Sharp was there. The City Marshal and Recorder were there. The police department was interested in the outcome of the case and so a number of police officers were in

---

[207] Baskin, *Reminiscences of Early Utah*, 229-30.
[208] "The Lascivious Charge," *Salt Lake Tribune*, Nov. 22, 1885.

attendance along with "[s]everal of the victims of the conspiracy."
[209]

Theodore Burmester and his partner, Enos Hoge, represented the defendant along with two other attorneys, Ben Sheeks and F.S. Richards. The latter, surprisingly, was the city attorney, an officer normally charged with prosecuting violations of the law not defending those accused of violating it! The Salt Lake Tribune said that this upside-down situation may seem incongruous, but "incongruities are to be looked for in this Latter-day kingdom."[210]

When the proceedings began, Enos Hoge challenged the entire venire, or jury panel, because, he argued, Marshal Elwin A. Ireland was prejudiced against the defendant. Hoge supported this proposition by asserting that the Marshal had formed and expressed an unqualified opinion as to the guilt of the defendant. Furthermore, Ireland had intentionally omitted to summon members of the Church of Jesus Christ of Latter-day Saints for jury duty. Marshal Ireland, Hoge claimed, knew very well that Hampton was a Latter-day Saint and so he summoned only jurors he thought were favorably predisposed to the prosecution, i.e. not Latter-day Saints.

---

[209] "Brig Roasted!" *Salt Lake Tribune*, Dec. 23, 1885, 4. Unless specifically noted, I have relied entirely on the reportage of the Salt Lake Tribune and the Deseret Evening News for facts concerning court proceedings and the trial testimony.
[210] Ibid.

Judge Zane overruled the defense objection out of hand, but when the prosecutor, Charles S. Varian, read the law to the Judge, demonstrating the Judge had to let the defense give evidence on the issue he withdrew his ruling and let the defense make their case. The lawyers made fairly technical arguments based largely on common law. But Hoge made the succinct claim that due to Ireland's prejudice he selected an entire panel of gentiles predisposed against his client—he did not claim a right to a panel of Latter-day Saints but rather a right to an impartial jury, one composed of all eligible men irrespective of religion. The prosecutors would rightfully object to a panel composed entirely of "Mormons", he argued. Judge Zane overruled the defense objection including the religious claim except as to the accusation that Marshal Ireland's selection was not impartial and so the defense called Ireland as a witness.[211]

Marshal Ireland testified that he had not picked any Mormons because he did not think that they would be impartial jurors. He selected men he thought would be "competent and worthy" and would render a just verdict.[212] Judge Zane denied the defense motion.

---

[211] "B. Y. Hampton's Trial," *Deseret Evening News*, Dec. 22, 1885.
[212] "Brig Roasted!" *Salt Lake Tribune*, Dec. 23, 1885.

Left to right: Associate Justice Powers; U.S. Marshal Ireland; Gov. Murray; Chief Justice Zane; U.S. Attorney Dickson; Associate Justice Boremen. Used by permission, Utah State Historical Society.

Theodore Burmester, Collection of the Author.

The Salt Lake Tribune reported by name each person in the venire who was questioned and named those who were excused due to challenge for bias and those who were challenged peremptorily. After ample questioning, the court and the parties were able to seat 12 jurors.[213] The court clerk then read the indictment "charging [the defendant with] conspiracy with Mrs. Fields to establish and maintain a house of ill fame in this city."

Varian "briefly stated the case" for the prosecution and then called his first witness, Mrs. S. J. Fields. The bailiff brought the forty-year-old woman into the courtroom from the Marshal's office, as she was a codefendant and had been brought back to the state from Colorado where she had fled. She wore a simple blue checked dress and a grey cloak. She tied a handkerchief over her head instead of a bonnet. Her "pale and haggard countenance" bespoke a "life of dissipation." The Salt Lake Tribune reported that "[h]er whole appearance suggested the propriety of her being employed as a tool of the Mormon church. A shade of anxiety and concern passed over Hampton's face as she came forward to be sworn…"[214]

As she took the stand, she trembled with fear. She was clearly being made a spectacle and woke up to discover she had been used by one side and was now being used by the other in a

---

[213] Ibid. The men selected as jurors on the case were: T. J. Almy, C. W. Lyman, J. P. Keate, J. M. Darling, Geo. W. Ellis, Samuel Paul, Isaac Hazelgrove, J. J. Duke, A. C. Brixod, T. E. Harper, Fulton Haigut, C. A. Dale.
[214] Ibid.

struggle for political power. She took her seat and the prosecutor began to ask her questions. However, to each question she sat mute staring at someplace far beyond the courtroom until Varian restated the question two or three times. Excited by the opportunity to rub the Latter-day Saints' collective noses in this scandalous mess, Mrs. Fields' reticence or inability to play the part that they so desired of her in this political theater, Varian, Judge Zane, and the jury quickly became frustrated with her.

Eventually, Mr. Varian was able to elicit from Mrs. Fields that she had lived in Salt Lake City in April through August of that year. She lived in a hotel until June when she moved into a house that she thought was across the street from the Continental Hotel on West Temple Street. After that she lived in a house next to Secretary Thomas.

At this point the testimony of the government's star witness hit a snag. Varian asked her why she had moved into the house next to Secretary Thomas when she did. Mrs. Fields answered somewhat incongruously, "I met Hampton before I moved into the house. He told me to go and see Mr. Butterfield and rent the house and he gave me the money to do it."[215]

---

[215] Ibid. The testimony laid out in the paper is strikingly complete, at least compared to the soundbites we get in newspapers and on television today. Nevertheless, it is not a transcript and sentences are abbreviated. I have tried to keep the sentences true to their substance from the newspaper while fleshing them out to make them sound more real. A further complication is that the newspaper reportage does not explain who certain peripheral characters are, like Mr. Butterfield.

From there it got worse. Varian would ask a question and Fields would only sit staring off into space. Varian would repeat the question, sometimes more than once, and Fields would finally reply, but often never directly answering the question posed. For example, Varian next asked, "This house you were to rent, what kind of house was that to be?"

To which Fields replied, "It wasn't my house; it was his."

The struggle continued: "What did he want you to do with the house he was to pay for? Were any names mentioned? Did he give you any money?"

"Yes, sir; he gave me money at different times. He gave me altogether about $400. I didn't keep any account, but he did."

"What was this money given to you for?" At first, Fields did not answer, did not even speak. Frustrated, Varian demanded an answer, "I'd like to have you answer the question."

Once again, a long silence ensued. Finally, as if she did not understand Varian's question she asked, "What was it given to me for?"

"Yes, that's the question." Another silence.

"Part of the money was given to me to pay for the house. Mr. Salmon and Mr. Smith (both policemen) came to me before I saw Mr. Hampton," she said as she pointed to Officer Salmon. "I met Hampton by appointment the second evening after that. . . . He said he wanted me to rent the house and work for him. He said their side had been punished. I understood he wanted to get the names of those parties just to keep them from sitting on juries. They reserved a room for themselves in the house."[216]

After Fields did not answer several more questions, the judge interjected "This witness seems to be an unwilling witness and the prosecution may put leading questions."[217]

Instead of asking a leading question, Varian merely pressed ahead, demanding an answer to his original question, "Mrs. Fields, you will please state what that house was to be used for."

But Fields clumsily dodged the question, "I don't know what it was to be used for. He hired me to work for him. I supposed men were to visit the house. He said he had a notion to go and hire a woman to work for him, but she didn't come, and he wanted me to work for him. I didn't understand that men were to be punished as they have punished them."

Throughout, Burmester and the defense team objected to the questions as fast as Varian could utter them.

The examination devolved into a hopelessly circular dance. Mr. Varian asked, "How did he want you to work for him?" When Fields did not answer, he restated his question more clearly, "What were you to do for him?"

---

[216] Ibid. The Salt Lake Tribune capitalized the words "KEEP THEM FROM SITTING ON JURIES" and set it out as a heading for emphasis.

[217] A leading question is one that suggests the answer and is normally not permitted with one's own witness on direct examination—unless the court finds the witness to be a "hostile witness."

However, it was not clarity of the question that held her back, and so she did not answer. Likely, she still felt some sense of loyalty to her former business partner and she did not yet realize he shared no such concern for her.

Finally, Varian demanded the court instruct his witness to answer the question. "Mrs. Fields you will answer the question or I shall hold you in contempt!"[218]

Slowly, haltingly, in a very low voice Mrs. Fields finally began to speak, "He, he smothered me up. He had all the witnesses and I had none." She paused, then continued, "they had a room and a key in both houses." She slowly shook her head as she said, "I never learned the names of all of them. I knew Salmon, he was there. And Hampton," she gave a nod toward the defense table, "he was there with Mr. Smith and Mr. Salmon. Their room was downstairs."

Feeling a little more confident, Varian asked, "What were they there for?"

Hurt and feeling trapped and yet still defiant, Fields answered, "they knew better than I do what they were there for. They were in that room themselves. I don't think it's right for me to be punished for somebody else as they have punished them."

Frustrated, Varian spat back, "That has nothing to do with this matter, now! Answer the questions! What were those rooms for, which were occupied by these men?"

---

[218] The newspaper did not quote the judge's instruction. This is my approximation.

Once again Fields gave a sideways answer, "I'd hear men come in and go out, but I did not see them every time."

Persistently returning to the point, Varian demanded, "What business did you carry on in the house next to Secretary Thomas's?" Pause. "Did you receive male visitors?

Finally, "Yes, sir."

"Did you solicit men to go there?"

"Yes; I sent two notes."

Varian lifted two documents from his table and confidently carried them over to Fields at the witness stand. When he showed her the first one, she acknowledged it was a note she had sent to Commissioner McKay. The second document she identified as an advertisement she had placed. Fields described how she had gone to McKay's office after sending the note in an unsuccessful bid to solicit him. She also told the jury how Hampton had taken her on a buggy ride to point out Governor Murray's office. He instructed her to go there the next day and solicit him as well. Which, she exclaimed to the jury, "I done just as he told me to!"

Varian shifted his examination of Fields to the housing arrangements. She told the jury a man named Fiddle rented the house for her, but he used a fictitious name: McCall. To furnish the house, Hampton instructed her to get furniture from Mr. Dinwoodey which she did. What's more, it was Hampton who paid for it all.

Nearing the climactic end to his examination Varian sought to go out with a flourish and so he returned to the central question of the case—but Fields went back to evading his questions.

"Did you keep a house as a house of prostitution or assignation?"

"I don't know the difference."

"As either? Did you keep a house of prostitution or assignation, either one?"

"I suppose it would be called a house of prostitution."

"Mrs. Fields, at the time you occupied the house did you prostitute yourself?" Varian asked matter-of-factly.

Fields hemmed and hawed and Varian resolutely repeated the question. And once again, Fields avoided answering it. She said, referring to Hampton, "He hired the house and he hired me."

Once again Hampton repeated the question, "Madam, at the time you occupied the house did you act as a prostitute yourself?"

Fields did not look up, neither did she answer. The court room was silent except for the rustling of anxious observers shifting and leaning forward in their seats. Varian continued to stare at his witness as he demanded, "Mrs. Fields, while you occupied that house did you not prostitute yourself?"

Still no response from Mrs. Fields. Only silence, waiting. Then finally, mercifully, she meekly answered, "Yes, sir."

Varian let the answer hang in the air before he turned—much relieved—and then returned to his chair, relinquishing his witness to the defense.

Ben Sheeks rose from his seat at the crowded defense table. On cross examination Fields elaborated on her previous testimony concerning her initial meeting with Hampton. She told the jury how she first met Hampton on the street. She later made an appointment to meet with Hampton through officers Smith and Salmon. On the appointed day, she met Salmon, Smith, and two other men who escorted her into a basement room. The four men followed her down into the subterranean meeting where Hampton sat, awaiting their arrival. During this, their second meeting, Hampton and Fields concluded their contract, the terms of which included the provision that Hampton promised to pay her $300 if she could get the Governor into the house. She admitted making out affidavits against the men who visited her house though denied Hampton paid her for them.

With regards to the second house, Hampton gave money to Salmon who in turn gave it to a man named Fiddler who lived in the house under the ruse that he was her husband.[219] Another woman named Lydia Bailey lived there at the same time as she did. Once the authorities shut down the house she moved first to California and then to Denver. Captain Greenman caught up with her there and brought her back to Salt Lake City.

---

[219] In direct examination the Tribune calls the man "Fiddle" while on cross examination the Tribune gives the name "Fiddler".

In his next line of questioning, Sheeks attempted to demonstrate that Fields had made a deal with the government to save herself from prosecution. The Salt Lake Tribune claimed that up to this point Fields had been very reluctant to testify and avoided direct answers. This was the first time she was publically confronted with the notion that she too was charged with the crime of running a house of prostitution. According to the Tribune this brought a visible change in Fields' demeanor and "[s]he was silent no longer."

"Didn't Marshal Ireland or Mr. Varian tell you that if you would testify in this case they wouldn't prosecute you?" Sheeks asked.

"No they didn't. But (with animation) the other side told me if I would start that house and run it, I wouldn't be arrested or fined for it." Her answer drew laughter throughout the court room.

Emboldened or angry, Fields became even more excited and talkative, volunteering information.

"I thought they wanted to get those names to keep them from prosecuting their men. When those men were drawn on the jury they intended to show them up and keep them off the jury. They wanted to get the Governor so they could get their men out of the Pen; they promised to keep me out of trouble, and now I have to suffer for their meanness."

Sheeks desperately fought to gain control of the witness and get her to stop talking. For a moment he succeeded. But when she started to think about how Hampton and his men had used her, she let loose with another round of unsolicited testimony and questions of her own. "It was their own house and not mine. Didn't they put up the money to furnish the house and start it?" she said, motioning toward Hampton and his associates.

Unbelievably, Sheeks meekly replied, "I don't know."

His answer further angered her, "Well, I know it! I don't think I ought to be punished for running *their* own house. They've been whippin' the devil around the bush, and I've got to suffer!"[220]

The defense resigned in abject failure and Varian once again took charge of the witness. Varian handed Fields the affidavits and asked her who had given them to her, and she pointed at Hampton. She repeated what she had earlier said, "They knew I didn't know what I was about. I didn't know they were going to prosecute those men. The Hampton men put up all the money. It's a whippin' the devil around the bush and it isn't right."

She went on in a loud voice disparaging Hampton and his men for their behavior. When Varian was finished the judge excused her and she stepped down off the witness stand. As she passed by Hampton, he looked up at her and "made a ghastly attempt to laugh, but looked very much as though seized with a fit of apoplexy."[221]

That was all for the first day—the judge ordered the jury sequestered in the Valley House for the night.

---

[220] Exclamation marks and emphasis are mine.
[221] "Brig Roasted!" *Salt Lake Tribune*, Dec. 23, 1885.

The next morning an even larger crowd was on hand for the second day of trial. Governor Murray and Mayor Sharp joined the observers in the gallery.[222] The Salt Lake Tribune reported that throughout the trial Brigham Young Hampton was smug and "sneering" at the state's witnesses. Toward some he even went so far as to cast curses, "Liar!"

Varian's first witness of the morning was Officer Salmon. On direct examination he testified that he was familiar with the first house which adjoined Secretary Thomas' house on West Temple Street. During the time between April and September he watched from a hidden perch inside the house as Mrs. Fields engaged in intercourse with other men. For her work he paid her $10 on one occasion. But he also saw Hampton pay her a number of times at the office or at the house. The largest sum he saw Hampton pay her was $150. They had also established a hidden observation room in the second house, the one across the street from the Continental Hotel. From that vantage he had seen not only Mrs. Fields engage in intercourse, but he had also seen her roommate, Lydia Bailey do the same.

Ben Sheeks handled the cross examination for Salmon who testified that when Hampton paid Fields, Salmon never heard anything mentioned about "keeping a house" in exchange for the

---

[222] There is some confusion regarding the date of the next two Salt Lake Tribune papers. Both are dated December 24 though it is clear one covers the second day of trial and the other the third day of trial. Perhaps it was an evening issue printed with the 24th date but intended to be read on the 25th as it refers to things taking place the day before.

money. The lawyers further pursued this weak and silly technicality on redirect and re-cross examination.

The government's next witness was another Salt Lake City Police Officer named Pickett. He too testified that he had been at the houses which Salmon had identified. And like Salmon, he watched from a hidden room as Fields, Bailey and one other woman had sexual intercourse with male visitors. Pickett also acknowledged that he knew Fields before any of this occurred because she was a prostitute who he had encountered as such in his duties as a police officer.

Varian next called Commissioner McKay who was the Commissioner of the Supreme Court. He claimed that on July 23 a young courier brought him a note which he identified in court. He replied to it on the back of the note and returned it to the sender. Soon a woman, who by then he knew as Fields because he saw her testify the day before, came to his office in response to his reply to the note. Varian offered the note as evidence and the defense objected. The Judge overruled the objection and it was admitted.[223]

The note, from Fields, asked McKay to "call on her at her house on West Temple Street." McKay's reply written on the back read, "Shall be busy after 4 o'clock and therefore, cannot see you unless you call before that hour."

---

[223] Neither paper states what the objection was. Perhaps it was hearsay, but it would likely be excepted from that rule as a statement by a coconspirator in furtherance of the conspiracy, which is exactly what the territorial supreme court held on appeal, *People v. Hampton*, 4 Utah 258, 265 (1886).

Following the admission of the note, McKay testified that Fields arrived about 2:00 o'clock and they discussed the note. As Varian asked McKay to tell the jury about their discussion, the Defense again objected, and again the judge overruled the objection.

"She came into my office," McKay told the jury, "and said, 'Is this Judge McKay?' I answered yes. She said her name was Mrs. Fields, and that she would like to see me privately. We went into a back room and she wanted the doors closed. I then asked her again what her business was. She said a mutual friend had sent her there to get some legal advice. She wished to know what the law of this Territory was in reference to keeping assignation houses. I asked her who sent her to me to get that kind of advice, and she refused to mention names. I told her I was not in the habit of giving advice on such matters, and such questions were offensive…"

According to McKay, Fields then apologized but then each recycled their same questions: he demanding to know who sent her; she refusing to tell but demanding to know what the law was regarding assignation houses. At first McKay did not answer her question but asked if she thought she could make that line of work pay. She said she could if the "Gentiles stood in with her" since she had heard that the "Mormons" were not too keen on prostitution. Finally, McKay told her that she could be sentenced to five years prison for prostitution and she turned and ran out.

P. H. Lannon was the next government witness. Lannon was "connected with a newspaper" in Salt Lake City when he received a note from Fields asking that he call on her regarding business. He went to the house she had next to Secretary Thomas's sometime around 3 or 4 o'clock on a warm clear day and asked her, how he could be of service to her. She told Lannon that she was not from Salt Lake City and that she was "fond of fun and had heard that" he was as well. Further, she told him that "she was going to have a beautiful woman from Denver in a few days." Lannon then "congratulated her on the prospects of having one beautiful woman in the house and wished her a good day."

John S. Scott was the first of several witnesses Varian would call to the witness stand who had been members of the Grand Jury that indicted Hampton, Mrs. Fields, and Mrs. Davenport. During the Grand Jury and against even the advice of Charles Varian, Hampton had insisted on testifying in his own behalf. At Grand Jury according to Scott, Hampton testified that "he had made an arrangement with Mrs. Fields and he had paid her something like $400."[224]

In an effort to show that this scheme was not a planned law enforcement operation, Varian called the City Attorney, F. S. Richards, who testified that he was unaware of any complaints alleging the operation of houses of ill-fame or persons visiting

---

[224] Other members of the Grand Jury who testified at trial were the foreman, Morris Evans, W. A. Pitt, and W. F. Raybould, who at the time of the trial had lost his voice and cold barely make himself heard. All of these witnesses testified in basic substance to the same facts as John Scott.

such houses on West Temple Street. Furthermore, he had never seen any complaints charging this sort of conduct.[225]

Varian called as his next witness, Frank Armstrong, a lumber merchant and Selectman for Salt Lake County. He began his testimony by acknowledging that he knew Brigham Young Hampton. Hampton had come to Armstrong and told him that there was a prostitution problem in their midst. So persuasive was his argument that he convinced Armstrong to donate $500 to help fund a private investigation that would help in the prosecution of the violators. However, he did not know this "detective scheme" would involve establishing a new brothel.

Henry Dinwoodey, the man from whom Fields claimed Fiddle—using the name McCall—had obtained furniture for the house, corroborated her testimony.

The next government witness, Justice Spires, was the police magistrate. He testified that several complaints had been filed in his court charging men with "visiting houses of ill-fame on West Temple street." All the complaints had been sworn to by two individuals. Varian showed Justice Spires one of those complaints which alleged that Mrs. Fields' house was a house of prostitution and that the defendant named in the complaint, a man named Pierson, apparently visited it. What made the document relevant was that it boldly asserted Hampton's connection to the house. It

---

[225] The next witness, Marshal Phillips, testified similarly.

was admissible because it was Hampton himself who had signed it attesting to its veracity.

The next two witnesses further corroborated Fields' testimony. M. L. Cummings, a real estate agent, confirmed he had rented the house next to Secretary Thomas's home to a man named McCall on July 3 but evicted the tenants the following month once he learned the house was being kept as a "house of assignation." Secretary Thomas himself said that there was short term traffic coming and going from the house next door and throughout the night "loud, profane and vile language" emanated from within its walls.

Finally, Varian recalled Officer Salmon who testified to the layout of the interior of the house and pointed out to the jury where the police had hidden themselves away to peep at Fields and her visitors. Hampton had been at Fields' house one night while Salmon was there (presumably both were witnesses hiding in the observation room).

Once the defense finished their second opportunity to cross-examine Salmon, Charles Varian faced Judge Zane and announced that Salmon had been the government's last witness and accordingly the "prosecution rests." Judge Zane adjourned the trial until 2:00 in the afternoon.

The Defense began its case when court resumed in the afternoon. Their first witness was a man named T. C. Armstrong, however, an early objection from Charles Varian cut the testimony so short that the Salt Lake Tribune's report of it makes no sense and the Deseret Evening News did not even report it.

Brigham Young Hampton Takes the Stand

According to the Salt Lake Tribune "[i]t was pretty generally understood" from the beginning what Hampton's defense would be and that Hampton would therefore have to testify, so when he was called to the witness stand there was no great stir of surprise in the gallery. Ben Sheeks conducted the direct examination and began by having Hampton tell the jury that he first met "Mrs. Fields between the 12th and 15th of [the previous] June [when] Mr. Salmon brought her to the jailor's house east of City Hall." Prior to that he claimed to have never seen her before. It was at that meeting when he entered into an agreement with Mrs. Fields to do "detective work." Their agreement, he explained, was that he promised to pay her $25 in exchange for every man caught in her house and for which she wrote an affidavit denouncing the man. He denied offering a special bounty for certain individuals. The offer was the same, "$25 for all, Mormon, Jew or Gentile…." This was the entirety of their agreement. He thought that she already had a house from which to pursue her part of the bargain. So, there was no need for other terms or to set up a home for Mrs. Fields. Indeed, he denied paying rent or furnishing either house for Fields or Davenport— "what money I paid her was for detective services."

Strangely, Sheeks and Hampton made the point that Evans' testimony (the foreman from the Grand Jury) was not accurate. To me this is strange because it is not the most damning evidence and because Hampton adopted Evan's assertions anyway. Sheeks asked him what his testimony was before the Grand Jury, and Hampton replied that he testified that he "knew Mrs. Fields and Mrs. Davenport and believed they kept houses of ill fame" though he did not know who rented or furnished the houses. He claimed that he had testified to the Grand Jury that he paid $300 to $400 to Mrs. Fields and that this money was strictly for "detective purposes."

Hampton could not have been completely unaware that his scheme had a serious legal flaw—that the men were being entrapped. Thus, when Hampton insisted that his contract with Fields was strictly for detective purposes yet admitted those services consisted of paying prostitutes to seek out and solicit men who were not already looking to engage in sexual intercourse in exchange for money, it strains credulity to suppose Hampton did not realize this was entrapment.

Hampton continued to insist under Sheeks' examination that he did not have control over the houses, direct or indirect. Thus, if he had testified at the Grand Jury that he had "opened these houses [he] made a mistake and did not mean it." Finally, he told the jury, he had never offered to pay Fields $300 to get Governor Murray as Fields had testified. And that was it.

Sheeks likely looked over his notes just to make sure he had asked all the questions he planned for his client and then informed Judge Zane he had nothing further for the witness. Sheeks returned to his seat at counsel table.

Charles Varian no doubt relished this opportunity to examine the antagonist in this public theater. Varian confidently stood up from his seat at the prosecution table to begin his cross examination. Varian wanted to start by gaining concessions from Hampton. So, first he got Hampton to admit that during the course of the entire detective scheme he handled around $1,000. He also admitted that he was not a police officer. Nevertheless, he did have many strong connections to the police department that enabled him to proceed in the scheme as if he were a police officer.

Varian looked Hampton in the eyes and asked him, "What was 'the [purpose] of this detective service'?"

Hampton's reply, unsurprisingly, was at odds with his actions. "[T]he object of the detective service was to detect crime, and to break up bawdy houses; it was to prevent sexual crime, and punish violators of the law."[226] Even if you limit the evidence to his admissions, Hampton paid women he knew to be prostitutes to carry out criminal acts in order to obtain the women's statements to be used against their customers after the fact. There was no prevention. He promoted prostitution in order to punish the men who patronized prostitutes. Today it is a common practice to use

---

[226] "The Hampton Case," *Deseret Evening News*, Dec. 23, 1885. "The object was to detect crime, work up those houses and places of resort and furnished rooms in order that they might be detected and prevented." "Pro Bono Publico," *Salt Lake Tribune*, Dec. 24, 1885.

prostitute decoys to ensnare those who solicit sex for money or drugs from them. But it is entrapment and unlawful for the police or their agents to hire prostitutes to solicit sex in exchange for money. It is just plain unconscionable for the police to encourage the prostitutes to complete the unlawful act so as to collect evidence of a crime that might not have occurred but for the "detective work." For Hampton to claim he was preventing crime is at the very least, disingenuous.

Varian then asked Hampton if he was familiar with a brothel known as "Kate Flint's"—to which Hampton replied in the affirmative. Hampton agreed that the afore-mentioned scheme anticipated rolling up this house of ill-fame. But when asked what steps he had taken to do it Hampton began blubbering, "We've not got that far yet."

Hampton insisted that this was a private scheme, paid for entirely from private sources. Indeed, Frank Armstrong had been the primary source of the money, approximately $750. Incredibly, he insisted that public officers were not involved, although just minutes before he had admitted that city police officers had participated in the scheme.

When Varian pressed Hampton to admit he had paid Fanny Davenport $700 and Mrs. Fields $300 to $400, having just testified that Armstrong contributed only $750, he was forced to admit that he had used some of his own money. Hampton excused himself by explaining that he expected to be paid back.

Hampton admitted to the jury that he and Salmon had directed the operational scheme. Varian pounced on Hampton's answer and forced Hampton to admit that Salmon was a city police officer under the direction of the city marshal, testimony that flew in the face of the explanation he had just given moments before, that this had been a "private scheme".

Varian pointedly reconfirmed Hampton's earlier direct testimony that he knew nothing about furnishing Mrs. Fields' homes for her and that indeed he had been out of town on July 31 when she had moved from the first house to the second house. Varian asked him if he had been in San Francisco at the time. Hampton agreed that he had, from July 2 to August 8. Varian then exposed to the jury the purpose of Hampton's trip to San Francisco: he had met with a woman there named Mollie Woodward and a man named Goldstone in order that he might arrange with Goldstone to bring Woodward to Salt Lake City to perform "detective work." Hampton sounded ridiculous when he desperately clung to his assertion that he was not opening any houses of ill-fame although his newly hired "detective" would be on the "outside" of any existing house.

Varian was on a roll. He attacked the heart of the defense's case:

"Q—What particular object had you in view when you arranged this scheme?

A—Catching men who were going to these houses and to furnished rooms and punishing them.

Q—Punishing women, too?

A—I suppose so. I haven't troubled the women much, though.

Q—You say you did not contemplate opening new houses of ill-fame?

A—No, sir.

Q—How did you expect to detect existing crime if you didn't contemplate going to a house already in existence or opening new ones?

A—We might have watched men go into the houses and then broken down the doors and caught them.

Q—Did you expect to do that in this case?

A—Yes, sir.

Q—Do you know of a single instance in which you did do it?

A—No, sir..."[227]

From there Hampton's testimony devolved into a blend of excuses and insistence that he was engaged in a grandiose crime fighting scheme. He expected others to collect the evidence adduced from encounters generated by a "great many women...scattered throughout the city." But then again, he was not sure where these "great many women" would take the men for the encounters. Eventually Varian pointedly asked Hampton whether the design of the scheme was to "induce certain individuals to commit these offenses for the purpose of exposing them?"

---

[227] "Pro Bono Publico," *Salt Lake Tribune*, Dec. 24, 1885. Interestingly, this exchange is not mentioned in the Deseret Evening News

To which Hampton strenuously replied, "No, sir."

Hampton's testimony once again fell into the same circle—the women were hired to be detectives not prostitutes. He did not open houses of "ill-fame." He did not know where his "detectives" were going to detect. Though the imported women were hired as detectives their statements were not the evidence they would use in court, rather they would use "their witnesses." The women were not prostitutes and he did not open a brothel.

Finally, Varian turned the witness back over to the defense. On redirect examination, Hampton explained the intent of his plan: "My plan was to catch the men, because men support these things." The scheme, he insisted was aimed at the "practice and not any particular houses." Hampton was excused and stepped down from the witness stand.

A curious incident followed the conclusion of Hampton's testimony. One of the jurors, Mr. Lyman, became ill and was assisted from the court room. Shortly thereafter a bailiff entered the court room to explain that Mr. Lyman was too sick to continue. Judge Zane asked the parties if they wished to continue without Mr. Lyman and only 11 jurors![228] Ed Hoge for the defense objected and suggested that the Court could allow "the case to go over for the term" so Mr. Lyman could recover. Judge Zane wanted the case to end as quickly as possible (some things never

---

[228] Ibid.; "The Hampton Trial," *Deseret Evening News*, Dec. 24, 1885. Both parties are entitled to a certain number of jurors, in this case 12, by statute or rule. It would violate due process to force a defendant to proceed without the full number of jurors.

change), and so he decided to adjourn until four o'clock (apparently only 30 minutes) in the afternoon and see if Mr. Lyman had recovered. Someone summoned a physician for Mr. Lyman. By four in the afternoon Lyman was feeling much better. The physician reported to the judge that it was the overcrowded courtroom that had caused Mr. Lyman's illness. Accordingly, Judge Zane ordered the court cleared of spectators and the trial resumed. The Deseret Evening News reported that the judge even ordered a couch be brought into the court room for Mr. Lyman.

The defense called E. L. Butterfield who testified that on June 3rd he had rented a house located across the street from the Continental Hotel to Mrs. Fields. I suppose that the purpose of the witness was to show it was Mrs. Fields and not Hampton who established the house. It is difficult without the full transcript. Either way it seems like a lot of work for little payoff, however.

The next witness that the defense called to the stand was "policeman" Bateman. He told the jury that he was acquainted with both Hampton and Mrs. Fields and was present when they entered their agreement sometime between June 12 and 15. She had claimed to have already obtained a house and wished to begin "detective work" immediately. The terms of the bargain were that Hampton would pay her $25 for each man "she caught in her house." But there was no agreement that Hampton would furnish the house. The defense attorney then relinquished the witness to Charles Varian for cross examination.

Bateman admitted that he was a Salt Lake City police officer at the time of the meeting. This was the first time Bateman had ever met Mrs. Fields and he recalled it was Salmon who spoke first. "This is the lady." According to Bateman, Mrs. Fields then explained she had come to "see about some detective business." Hampton said he wanted to "catch men who were visiting the houses of prostitution." Mrs. Fields accepted the job. Under this agreement Mrs. Fields was to make affidavits for each man and Hampton would pay her $25 for each one. Bateman testified he did not hear anyone say where Mrs. Fields was to go or who she was to catch. He conceded that it was likely decided at some earlier meeting. Bateman then testified that Hampton later ordered Bateman to go to Mrs. Fields' house to witness acts of prostitution on at least two occasions. This last assertion is inconsistent with the rest of his and Hamilton's testimony. Neither he nor Hampton claimed to know where the woman was conducting her business, yet Hampton ordered Bateman to go to a location he knew nothing of, to observe a crime without being detected—an impossible task without a vantage point on the inside, which of course would require a prior agreement and alteration of most houses. Why hire a detective to produce affidavits that were not going to be used according to Hampton? And why did a police officer respond to an order from a civilian to go watch a crime through to consummation.

Once Varian finished his cross examination of Policeman Bateman, the defense recalled Brigham Young Hampton who declared in obvious response to the cross examination of Bateman, that the meeting Bateman testified to, was the only time Hampton entered into any agreement.[229]

The Defense then rested, and the trial ended for the day. The Court scheduled the parties to make closing arguments in the morning and limited each side to two and a half hours.[230] According to the Deseret Evening News, Mr. Lyman was allowed to go home for the night while the rest of the jury was again sequestered at the Valley House.

Closing Arguments

The next morning Mr. Lyman felt well enough to continue and the defense confirmed they did not intend to call any further witnesses. Thus, the parties closed the case for taking evidence. All that remained was final argument and charging the jury. Judge Zane turned to the prosecutor and instructed him to proceed with his closing argument.

Charles Varian pushed his chair back from his table and stood. I can imagine that he slowly but purposefully walked to the center of the well, all the time his head lowered deep in thought. Then suddenly he would have looked up, briefly turned to the judge and begun, "Your honor," turning to the defense table, "Counsel," then back to the jury box, "Gentlemen of the jury. Brigham Young Hampton entered into a conspiracy with his two

---

[229] Ending with a whimper, the defense called for their last witness, Captain Greenman who testified that he went to Denver to arrest Fields.

[230] That is an amazing figure. I recall a judge limiting me to 45 minutes (30 for closing and 15 for rebuttal) in a murder case!

confederates, Mrs. Fields and Mrs. Davenport. The object of their conspiracy was keeping a house of ill-fame and the people have proved their case against the defendant beyond a reasonable doubt."[231]

Conspiracy at common law required that the government provide some corroborating evidence of the conspiracy before the jury could accept the testimony of the co-conspirator, in this case Mrs. Fields, the government's star witness. Thus, Varian had to explain this legal quirk, and then proposed that the jury accept the reverse—once corroborating evidence had been offered, the jury ought to then accept Mrs. Fields' testimony in full.

Reviewing the evidence, Varian reminded the jury that the defendant himself admitted he entered into a scheme with several persons to "detect sexual crime." Despite active city and county governments with able police forces the defendant and several other private persons undertook this public enterprise in secret. There were, at the time, a fair number of brothels in operation and well known to the community. Nevertheless, the defendant did not proceed against these "most offensive" houses. Rather, "[t]he scheme was commenced by rounding up houses which did not exist, or which were opened for the purpose...[this] scheme...had not the sanction of the law, but was to make the good bad, and the bad worse...The law did not contemplate the commission of crime

---

[231] "The Hampton Trial," *Deseret Evening News*, Dec. 24, 1885.

for the detection of criminals." "It was beneath the dignity of any government to lead men into crime in order to suppress it."[232]

"How can that man get on the witness stand here and swear before his maker that he did not contemplate the opening of houses of ill-fame?" Varian asked rhetorically. Hadn't Hampton testified that he had paid prostitutes to come to the city to ply their trade in order to "detect crime." How were these women to do their business? Where were they to live? And yet he claimed to not have opened a house of ill-fame?

The jury could safely accept the testimony of Mrs. Fields because her testimony was corroborated by the Grand Jury testimony of the defendant himself. In essence, his own "testimony before the Grand Jury sealed his fate. The evidence was complete, and the defendant had bound himself in his own toils and stood a convicted criminal."[233] The Deseret Evening News reported that Varian closed by pointing out the pink elephant in the court room, that the money used to finance the scheme was drawn from one class and then "directed against another class[.]"

Clearly, he intended to indict Hampton's plan as one organized by Latter-day Saints against gentiles. However, that is precisely the same argument, merely in reverse, that Enos Hoge complained of at the beginning of the trial, that no Latter-day Saints were allowed to participate in the jury pool to even have the

---

[232] Ibid.

[233] "Brig's Christmas Gift," *Salt Lake Tribune*, Dec. 24, 1885.

possibility of being selected—an attack on Latter-day Saints by gentiles. The scenario raises the question whether the situation was so partisan to be in essence an insurgency, such that no Latter-day Saint could be trusted to sit in judgment of another Church member.

As Varian returned to his seat, Enos Hoge stood and began the closing argument for the defense. He first attacked the testimony of Mrs. Fields, because, as he reminded the jury, under the law if her testimony was not corroborated then the jury could not accept any of her testimony regarding the conspiracy. Despite her testimony that the details of the agreement were reached regarding Hampton's involvement in the scheme she could not recite a single statement that his client ever made during their meeting. He pointed out that the notes brought into court from Mrs. Fields to McKay and Lannon had no evidentiary connection to Mr. Hampton. He then pointed out little inconsistencies in the details of the testimony of each of the Grand Jurors regarding Hampton's Grand Jury testimony. Hoge then reminded the jury what Varian had said at the end of his closing, intimating that this was a dispute between classes (Latter-day Saints and gentiles). Hoge asked the jury if his client was to be held responsible for the actions of his "class"? or was Varian encouraging them to succumb to their own base prejudices?

Hoge then contrasted Hampton's testimony and manner with that of Mrs. Fields in order to demonstrate to the jury that they ought to believe Hampton over Mrs. Fields. And then, Enos

Hoge went back to the class argument—Hampton was a Latter-day Saint and the jury was not—and in accordance, the jury ought not hold that against him.

In conclusion, Hoge returned to the "class" theme one more time. The prosecution, he claimed, had chided Hampton for claiming to be fighting crime. Yet it was this same prosecutor who had failed to effectively combat prostitution, because he did not prosecute those (that class, gentiles) who visited prostitutes. He accused the prosecutor of arguing that prostitutes could not be believed as against the other class (gentiles). He then drew them back to the class distinction at hand—gentile jury and Latter-day Saint accused—and told them he did not urge them to believe either side due to class alone. Rather, "[a]ll that the defendant asked was that the testimony be impartially weighed, and give a verdict thereon."[234]

The court recessed for lunch until 2:00 PM.

Once the jury returned, Theodore Burmester stood to address the jury.

> [I] had expected to hear from the prosecution a clear statement of the facts in the case, but [was] disappointed. [I t]hought he would have done so in fairness to the counsel for the defense, to the court, and to the people, but he [did] not. [I am] appalled and humiliated by having to listen to talk from the prosecution that might have been proper in a police court. There [is] no occasion for a tirade of abuse. Feeling and epithets [do] not constitute argument. A [prosecutor] should never stoop to personal

---

[234] "The Hampton Trial," *Deseret Evening News*, Dec. 24, 1885.

abuse and I [am] amazed at hearing it. A bare statement of the indictment and an explanation of its terms were all that was necessary, so that the matter could be simplified. [Brigham Young] Hampton was accused of conspiracy with Mrs. Fields, alias Mrs. McCall alias Miss Harris, to commit a crime against the people of the Territory of Utah, in that they agreed to keep and maintain a house of ill-fame. [You, the jury were] selected for [your] especial fitness to try this case impartially, and [you] should do so intelligently. The argument of the prosecutor tended to confuse instead of enlighten. . . . A conspiracy [is] an unlawful combination of two or more persons, by concerted action, to commit an unlawful means to accomplish an act not unlawful in itself. There was no such combination in this case. There was no evidence of the agreement charged. Mrs. Fields said she was hired to work for defendant. If this were true, there was no conspiracy in it. Mr. Hampton testified that he hired the woman for detective purposes. That was all there was of it, and no jury could make a case of conspiracy out of it. It was simply a case of *hiring* a person to do certain work for detective purposes. The testimony all agreed that the woman was hired and was to be paid $25 for each person caught. There was no occasion for abuse or invective. The agreement was made, and money paid for the detection of crime, not its commission. A great deal had been said of a war between classes, but with that the defendant had nothing to do. He alone was on trial. The question of the veracity of witnesses in another case had nothing to do with this case. There was no reason for the prosecutor's attack on the city and county governments. The defendant had nothing to do with that. If the city and county had failed to prosecute certain crimes, so had the third jurisdiction, the prosecution in this court, and pot had no excuse for calling the kettle black; it was simply a division of the honors, and the defendant had no connection with it. The prosecution had also laid great stress upon the "moral" phase of the case—the allurements offered to men. Mrs. Fields had failed to allure the glorious triumvirate which had been referred to. This failure was in keeping with Mr. Hampton's statement that it was the detection of crime. All the testimony went to show that this was the full intent of the defendant, and that he had no idea of committing crime, and did not do so. Mrs. Fields had perjured herself, as Captain Greenman's testimony had shown. [I] have never witnessed, in all [of my] experience, such an exhibition of regard for the public welfare as Mr. Hampton had shown. When he was notified before the grand jury that he could decline to testify, he refused to take advantage of any technicality, and volunteered to tell the whole truth. The detective business was an ungrateful one at the best, and in the present case the ingratitude was most glaring. It was a well-known fact that this class of crime was difficult to detect. The defendant had hired detectives to ferret out the crime, and was fully justified in doing what he did, and he should not be convicted of a crime he did not commit, simply because he belonged to a certain class of people.[235]

Theodore Burmester returned to his seat and relinquished the well to the prosecution. Mr. Varian stood and once again engaged the jury with a "short, vigorous and dignified speech," according to the Salt Lake Tribune. His first order of business was to address the defense's accusations of his alleged unethical conduct by telling the jury he would not address the defense's accusations! Thus, moving on to the substance of his argument, Varian restated that Hampton was charged with criminal

---

[235] "The Hampton Trial," *Deseret Evening News*, Dec. 24, 1885. Although there is no indication that Theodore's closing argument was offensive or improper based on the reportage by the Deseret Evening News, the Salt Lake Tribune reported that "Mr. Burmester elaborated on the moral aspects of the case with a great deal of vulgarity and obscenity which is not fit for publication." "Brig's Christmas Gift," *Salt Lake Tribune*, Dec. 24, 1885.

conspiracy. A criminal conspiracy is as "[I] understand it, a corrupt and unlawful agreement to do some unlawful act[.] Whether one of the parties was hired by the other was immaterial. The ultimate object was inconsequent. The keeping of a bawdy house was in itself a crime, no matter what the object for which it was kept."[236] The defendant had gone to the house in which Mrs. Fields had set up her business in order to inspect it and must therefore have known its purpose as a house of ill-fame. Hampton had declared he did not "contemplate the opening of a house of ill-fame" but hadn't he intended to punish men for seeking the services of prostitutes? Rather than rounding up houses already in existence, Hampton had rounded up more prostitutes in California and brought them to Salt Lake City. "Judging from the evidence as a whole the scheme included enticing and alluring people, the old and the young, from the path of virtue…The sole object was not to detect and punish existing crime. Were there no other crimes in the Territory at that time? Why was not the attention of the conspirators called to the very prevalent crime of polygamy and the kindred offense, unlawful cohabitation? Why was it, if they were simply animated by a desire to suppress crime, we did not find them raising their voices in behalf of the American Union and the laws of their country, contributing their money and support of the enforcement of those laws? About a year ago when a call was made for all law abiding citizens to array themselves on the side of

---

[236] "Brig's Christmas Gift," *Salt Lake Tribune*, Dec. 24, 1885.

the law, where was Brig Hampton?...What excuse or vindication can there be for any man who ever nursed at woman's breast, who possessed any of the instincts of humanity, for entering into a scheme for dragging men from virtue and morality down to crime and shame?"[237]

Finally, Varian ended by protesting accusations made by the defense regarding his personal motivations.

The Salt Lake Tribune complained that Mr. Varian had not objected to the defense during their closing argument though they "stray[ed] far from the evidence," yet they had not extended him the same courtesy. Apparently, the defense frequently interrupted Varian with remarks and objections. However, as I read the reportage of both parties' arguments it seemed to me that it was the government in its rebuttal argument that strayed far from the evidence. When Varian called the jury's attention to what had occurred "about a year ago..." had nothing to do with any evidence adduced during the course of the trial. Indeed, a reference such as this, to the still simmering dispute between the Church of Jesus Christ of Latter-day Saints and the U.S government regarding polygamy was, especially given the makeup of the jury, explosively, and importantly, unfairly prejudicial.

The judge then charged the jury and sent them to a room to deliberate. Forty-five minutes later, just before 6:00 pm Bailiff Hurd told Judge Zane "that the jury 'were ready.'"

---

[237] Ibid.

Judge Zane replied, "Bring them in."

The jury filed back into the court room and took their seats. The foreman, Thomas J. Almy, handed the verdict to the clerk of the court who read from it: "The People of the Territory of Utah vs. B. Y. Hampton. Conspiracy. We, the jury in the above case find the defendant guilty of the crime of conspiracy, as charged in the indictment." The verdict must have elicited a collective gasp from the audience. However, an experienced judge like Judge Zane quickly would have reasserted control. Zane set the case for sentencing on Tuesday December 29. Meanwhile, Hampton was allowed to remain out of custody on bail.

The Salt Lake Tribune apparently contacted the jurors afterward and learned that the jury had cast three ballots in which they split 11-1 in favor of conviction on the first two. On the third ballot the lone hold-out changed his vote from acquittal to conviction and Brigham Young Hampton was convicted of Conspiracy.

The parties returned to the courtroom on December 29 for sentencing. However, Theodore began the proceedings by arguing for an arrest of judgment based on a claim that there was no crime of "conspiracy" to keep a house of ill-fame under the law. Theodore argued the matter at considerable length, but to no avail. Judge Zane overruled the objection and Mr. Sheeks switched places with Theodore at the podium and asked to proceed to sentencing. He then proffered the certificates of Dr. W. F. Anderson and Dr. Benedict averring that Brigham Hampton was ill with pleuropneumonia and if sentenced to confinement in prison his illness could turn fatal. Mr. Varian of course opposed the defense argument for lenience due to the defendant's ill-health. After all, the defendant appeared to be in full vigor of life, he argued. Moreover, such an argument as the defense was making tends toward a slippery slope where one convicted of murder might argue for leniency simply because he had contracted a cold. The judge took the argument under advisement until later in the morning and asked the defense to bring the physicians prepared to testify.

At ten o'clock the defense brought in three expert witnesses, physicians all, to testify why Hampton ought not be imprisoned. Dr. Benedict, Dr. W.F. Anderson, and Dr. S.O.L. Potter testified that Brigham Young Hampton suffered from pleuropneumonia and that in their opinion it would be hazardous to his health to place him in a cramped, dark humid environment like a jail.

Judge Zane then gave his findings and imposed sentence. First, he told those assembled in the court room that he was not convinced by either the certificates of the physicians or their testimony. Indeed, it was his opinion that the physicians had been reckless in their willingness to utter them. The testimony of the physicians he found to be inconsistent with each other and some not based on any examination of the defendant. Accordingly, he did not find sufficient cause for concern for the defendant's health such that confinement should be avoided.

Turning his focus entirely on the defendant Judge Zane then said, "The offense with which you are charged, Mr. Hampton, is one of course, that every right-minded man must condemn, according to your own statements. No man can enter into a partnership with a prostitute and be honored; and according to your own statement, you employed this miserable prostitute, as the evidence shows, to give her $25 for each man that she might make an affidavit against…but to employ detectives of bad character, such as prostitutes, to commit crimes themselves, and induce others to commit crimes, in order that they may be punished, brings disgrace and infamy upon the community and scandal upon society, involving families into trouble, and is a conspiracy to do that which deserves the deprication [sic] and condemnation of all decent men. No man that does this ought to ever, until he reforms, go out among decent people and hold up his head. Your conduct, as shown by this evidence, leads me to believe that you are so lost to all sense of propriety and decency that, I confess, I feel like giving you a severe punishment. The interest of society, the good of society, demands particularly that this crime against chastity, in this community, should be punished severely....There was no necessity to import prostitutes from other cities, from hundreds of miles. It is better to get rid of what we have got....The object [of the criminal law] is to make the punishment certain and definite, in order that it may be a terror to others. I therefore, under these circumstances, do not choose to impose a fine in this case. As you seem to be the leader in this matter, this new phase of crime that seems to have developed here among many others, and which seems to be degrading and disgracing and weighing down this community, I will give you the full benefit of the law. You will be sentenced to imprisonment in the county jail for the term of one year." The judge then told Hampton that if his physical health was a problem then he should tell the governor, "clemency resides" with him. And then for good measure after a moment's pause, Judge Zane added that costs of the proceedings were charged to the defendant.

Enos Hoge then asked the judge to allow Hampton to remain on bail pending his appeal to the Territorial Supreme Court. Varian objected of course and Judge Zane replied to Hoge that it was the court rule that no one would be allowed bail in any case [after sentencing] unless they demonstrated good reasons for the privilege. Hoge argued that the testimony of the physicians was good reason.[238] Judge Zane denied the defendant's motion and Hampton was taken into custody.

The news of Hampton's conviction was reported in newspapers as far away as New York City.[239]

Hoge, Burmester, Sheeks, and Rawlins immediately appealed to the Territorial Supreme Court. That court heard the case and published an opinion in January 1886. Unimaginably, Judge Zane as Chief Justice, sat on the three-justice panel that

---

[238] Note that he did not seek a delay, unlike the appellate docket of today, Hoge expected that the Territorial Supreme Court would hear the case and decide it by the next month. "Taken to Jail," *Salt Lake Tribune*, Dec. 30, 1885.

[239] See "The Mormon Conspiracy," *New York Times*, Dec. 31, 1885.

reviewed his decisions during the trial! Not surprisingly the appellate court affirmed the conviction. Most of the issues were fairly easy regarding sufficiency of the jury instructions and the admissibility of Fields' note to Commissioner McKay. In my view, the only troubling issue was the jury selection question. The court's decision that a defendant does not have an absolute right to a jury composed at least in part of members of the Church of Jesus Christ of Latter-day Saints by itself is sound, but it ignores that the members of the panel were selected for jury duty *because* they were not Latter-day Saints. To put it a different way, law abiding citizens were deprived of their right to serve on a jury because of their faith. Today the analysis has shifted from the defendant's right to a certain jury composition to the infringement of a citizen's right to participate in the democratic process by potentially serving on a jury.[240]

Brigham Young Hampton served his year in jail.[241] Soon after he got out of jail, he found himself involved in similar legal troubles. Hampton owned a building and leased it to Louis Bamberger a German Jew who along with his brothers were important Salt Lake businessmen. They in turn sublet the building to Elsie Omar who opened a brothel.[242] However, Varian

---

[240] *See Batson v. Kentucky*, 476 U.S. 79 (1986).
[241] Presumably Mrs. Fields' charges were dropped in exchange for her cooperation. Fanny Davenport, the other "detective" charged in the conspiracy, escaped to Canada with the assistance of Hampton's confederates. Nichols, *Prostitution*, 34.
[242] Nichols, *Prostitution*, 89.

dismissed the charges because Hampton had nothing to do with this particular house of prostitution.

Chapter 9: Epilogue

Following the conclusion of the Hampton trial and its subsequent appeal, Theodore continued to practice law in both Salt Lake and Tooele counties. Throughout his career his case load consisted predominantly of collections actions with the occasional criminal case. He continued to maintain this same case composition while he lived and worked in Utah. During the 1880s in Salt Lake City he operated two collection agencies at different times. At the same time, he was also active in real estate transactions, particularly in Tooele County. He bought 160 acres in 1882; another 160 in 1884; and more transactions followed. Then in 1892 he unloaded 1600 acres.

After marrying for the third time he and his last wife, Maria Finch, began having children. Though all the children except the last were born in Grantsville in Tooele County, Theodore always maintained an office and residence in Salt Lake City. He moved into and out of several houses in downtown Salt Lake City during the 1880s until he moved into a house just off South Temple Street, 8 blocks east of Main Street. [243]

Following the Bingham bar room gun fight in the early 1870s, Theodore's brother, William, left Utah for Stevensville, Montana. Initially he had some success there in mining, but like most miners he ultimately realized precious little success for all

---

[243] Pursuant to Brigham Young's original city plan Salt Lake was measured in blocks from the Temple Square. Main Street is the eastern boundary to the square while South Temple is the southern boundary.

his efforts at prospecting. Then while still a young man of only 43 years of age William died of dropsy on August 15, 1883.[244]

John Rogers McBride, one of Theodore's defense attorneys in the Morford homicide case and who later testified in Congress against Utah statehood continued to be active in Republican politics and the practice of law in Salt Lake City. As the century pressed to a close, he retraced his steps back to the west, first to Boise and finally to Spokane, Washington where he died on July 20, 1904.

Major Romily Foote, the lead prosecutor in the Morford homicide case and sometime running partner of Theodore, proved to be somewhat of an enigma. On June 13, 1866 Foote was the 24th man admitted to the newly established Idaho Territory Bar. Though the territory was created in 1863 it took the next three years to create, appoint, and convene the Territorial Supreme Court. The court finally convened on May 31, 1866 and its "first order of business was to admit H.L. Preston, [Joseph Rosborough's eventual partner] as an attorney and counselor of the Court."[245] Theodore and several others were admitted on June 1, 1866.

Foote remained in the territory to report on the 1870 census that he lived in Boise and possessed $300 in personal assets. He claimed to have been born in Mississippi though I have

---

[244] Obituary, *Missoulian* (Missoula MT), August 31, 1883.
[245] Debra K. Kristensen, "The First 50 Men in Idaho Law," *The Advocate*, 55 (October 2010).

not been able to find any corroborating information to that effect in Mississippi state records or Confederate Army records. He is not entered on the 1880 census. The Idaho Bar rolls list him as deceased as of September 1881.[246] He would have been 38 years old.

The other prosecutor on the Russell Morford homicide, Ned Holbrook, told Thomas Donaldson his greatest fear was to be shot in the back—I don't know if that reveals a guilty conscience or just a plain irrational fear because being shot in the back can't hurt any more than the front. Though it remains unknown whether Holbrook suffered from a guilt-ridden conscience or paranoia, he was nevertheless, as it turns out, prophetic. A man named Charles Douglas shot Holbrook in the back just outside Ned's office six months after Theodore's trial. Like Theodore, the jury acquitted Douglas in a trial presided over by the very unpopular Judge Noggle.[247]

Newspaper editor, James Reynolds, met and fell in love with a young woman from California who was visiting along with her mother, sometime before John Konapeck attacked Ariminta. Reynolds married the young lady in 1868.[248] However, after only three years his wife left him. Reynolds was crushed. He suddenly sold the Idaho Tri-Weekly Statesman on January 2, 1872.[249] With

---

[246] Ibid., 60.
[247] Donaldson, *Idaho of Yesterday*, 146.
[248] Ibid., 129.
[249] *James S. Reynolds*, Idaho State Historical Society Reference Series, no. 593 (1981).

an obsessive single-mindedness, he hunted the woman down in California where, Thomas Donaldson cryptically writes that, Reynolds "found the girl and her mother in an out-of-the-way place, one winter night. Certainly a trajic [sic] scene was enacted there. Jim considered himself fortunate in escaping with his life; two of his predecessors in the woman's affections were not as fortunate."[250]

Henry Prickett, Theodore's lawyer to whose office he ran to get away from Russell Morford the night before the shootout, stayed in Boise after the trial. He was important to the community there as a problem solver. In November 1867 he stepped in as Boise's first mayor—the elected mayor refused to take office in protest against the charter that incorporated the city.[251] He stayed in office only two months to get things going and resigned in January 1868. In 1876 he was appointed to the Territorial Supreme Court and was tasked with organizing all the court's decisions from 1866 into a new Idaho Reports. Prickett retired from the bench in 1884 and returned to private practice. On June 14, 1885 Prickett was in Hailey Idaho attending court. When he did not appear that morning for court his partner went to check on him in his room. His partner discovered that, he was dead, having died quietly in his sleep, in bed.[252]

---

[250] Donaldson, *Idaho of Yesterday*, 130.
[251] Kristensen, "The First 50 Men," 58.
[252] "Sad News of Judge Prickett's Death," *Idaho Tri-Weekly Statesman*, Jun. 16, 1885.

Theodore's two main lawyers in the Morford homicide case were Joseph Rosborough and Frank Ganahl. They visited Salt Lake City together and presumably spent time with Theodore and McBride. Rosborough left Boise and was dropped from the bar rolls by 1881.[253] Ganahl, the great orator, remained in the area. During a break in a trial somewhere near present-day Coeur d'Alene Ganahl was joking around with his opposing counsel, W. B. Heyburn, who like Ganahl was a large man in height and girth. Heyburn called Ganahl fat to which Ganahl replied, "I carry my fat under my belly band, where a gentleman should, and not under my hat band, where my friend does."[254] Frank Ganahl died in Spokane, Washington in 1898.[255]

Frank Burmester was the only child of Theodore and Ariminta to survive into adulthood. As a young man Frank worked his father's ranch in Tooele County called the Minnehaha. Later, he pursued several business opportunities, real estate, mining and livery. He was credited with successfully coaxing a subsidiary of the Diamond Match Company to build a potash plant at the edge of the Great Salt Lake near the Grants Railroad station on the Western Pacific line.[256] Potash, or Potassium Sulfate, was used in artillery munitions propellant, which in 1916 at the height of

---

[253] Ibid., 60.
[254] "Ganahl the Orator," *Idaho Legal History Society Newsletter*, 1, no. 2, (Oct. 2009): 3; Nelson Wayne Durham, *History of Spokane and Spokane County*, (Spokane: The S. J. Clarke Publishing Co., 1912) 490.
[255] "Recent Deaths," *The American Lawyer*, 6 (1898): 309.
[256] Ouida Blanthorn, *A History of Tooele County*, (Salt Lake City: Utah State Historical Society, 1998), 322.

World War I was a "booming" business. The potash plant led to the birth of the town of Burmester nearby, albeit short lived. Frank's livery business delivered goods from the rail station at Grants to Grantsville. A remnant of this history can be found today in the road—that runs from Grantsville due north to I-80 where Grants station was—called "Burmester Road." Frank was later elected a Republican mayor of Grantsville for several terms.

Frank Burmester, Collection of the Author.

Interestingly, Joshua Reuben Clark Sr. recorded in his diary an encounter that he attributed to Frank, but I think was actually Theodore. The casual way in which he records the events of April 21, 1888 is worth reading in its entirety.

> Saturday. April. 21st. 1888.
> A warm day. I sheared three more sheep for Elmer to-day, and after Reuben finnished [sic] plowing and I got my dinner I took the George horse up

town, and got Richard Robinson, to put Some
Shoes on him. Parley Kimball and Frank
Burmester, had a trial this afternoon Burmester
was fined ten dollars and costs for drawing a
revolver on Kimball and threatening to Shoot him.
A.G. Johnson and myself go on a mission
tomorrow to Lakeview. The grain is needing
water very bad.[257]

Though Clark knew Theodore and referred to him by his
name elsewhere in his diary I think he was mistaken because I
have found no other evidence Frank ever acted as a lawyer and no
evidence that Frank was a hot-head with a proclivity for drawing
guns during arguments. Of course, Theodore had a history of both.

Joshua Reuben Clark Sr. began his diary January 22, 1862
at about the time he joined the army after the start of the Civil
War. After the war he and several other young men made a long
cold ride to Utah. He finally reached Salt Lake City March 11,
1867. He was instantly enamored by the Church of Jesus Christ of
Latter-day Saints and had himself baptized on April 14 that same
year.

In addition to knowing Theodore Burmester, Clark was a
close acquaintance of John Quincy Knowlton. Like Clark,
Knowlton was a Latter-day Saint. He was also a polygamist and
another of my great-great-grandfathers; my paternal
grandmother's grandfather. Knowlton and his three wives and
many children lived on a large ranch in Skull Valley in Tooele

---

[257] Clark, "Journal Transcriptions," April 21, 1888.

County.[258] Clark described the July 24, 1881 "Days of '47" celebration in Grantsville. There was a parade, speeches, music, and children's dance. The adults partied late into the night, racing horses and drinking alcoholic beverages. Knowlton and six or seven other men piled into a carriage driven by "bro[ther] Worthington." All had imbibed too heavily in Clark's estimation. Consequently, the men were impaired when they went speeding around a corner. The driver lost control of the carriage and it tipped over, tossing all the occupants out on to the ground. Amazingly, no one died although several of the men were slightly injured.[259]

John Quincy Knowlton's third wife, Mary, had originally come from England to marry his brother. The man had met Mary while proselytizing as a missionary for the Church of Jesus Christ of Latter-day Saints there. However, before they could marry, he died. Eventually, John Quincy took her on as his third wife and she joined his other families at the ranch in Skull Valley.[260]

Mary and John Quincy had 7 children. Their eldest was a daughter also named Mary but was known to all as "Mame." However, in 1886 after Mame had moved out of the house Mary became very ill with breast cancer though she still had young children living at home. In early December John Quincy went into the mountains to hunt. I don't know if he realized how close to

---

[258] Clark, "Journal Transcriptions," August 7, 1880.
[259] Clark, "Journal Transcriptions," July 25, 1881.
[260] Maurine Griffith Burmester, interview by Jeanne Bryan Inouye and Lois Griffith Bryan, May 11, 1997, transcript in possession of the author.

death Mary was or if the trip shows how desperate his families were for the game he expected to kill, but on December 11, 1886 while he was still gone she succumbed to the cancer at 52 years of age.[261] Word of her passing was sent out immediately to John Quincy. Upon hearing the terrible news, he drove his horse hard toward the rail station at Deseret. During this frantic flight John Quincy was thrown from his horse. Unlike the carriage crash, in this fall he was hurt seriously, breaking three ribs and likely driving them into his lung. Others tried to help him get to medical treatment, but he was in the wilderness 100 miles south of Grantsville and he died after 12 hours of agonizing pain.[262] Joshua Reuben Clark Sr. reported in his diary on December 14, 1886 that he had received word that John Quincy had died. Clark wrote that Mary was in Salt Lake City, perhaps in a hospital when she died.

The sudden death of John Quincy left three families without a father and one without father or mother. At the time Mame was 21 years old and upon her was set the responsibility of taking care of herself and her six siblings. According to my Grandmother, John Quincy had borrowed a large sum of money from the Church of Jesus Christ of Latter-day Saints for the ranch. When he died, the Church took over the ranch. The wives still living were forced to move to Salt Lake City to live with their

---

[261] Obituary, *Deseret News Weekly*, 35, no. 48 (Dec. 15, 1886): 762.
[262] "Local News," *Deseret News Weekly*, 35, no. 49 (Dec. 22, 1886):776. Initially the Deseret News Weekly reported that John Quincy had collapsed and died from grief after hearing that Mary had died.

children. Mary's young children were forced to leave the ranch as well. They all moved in with Mame who had to raise them.[263]

John Quincy Knowlton, Collection of the Author.

Tragedy and duty fully defined poor Mame's life. She was engaged to marry when her fiancé was murdered while in Idaho. Charles Griffith went to her home to tell her the sad news. After that auspicious meeting Charles and Mame later fell in love and married. They had seven children including my grandmother, who was only four years old when Charles, a supervisor at American Smelter and Refining, fell from a trestle, crushing his skull. Once again Mame was forced to raise a family of children on her own.[264]

Thomas Corwin Iliff worked tirelessly trying to grow the Methodist Church and fighting polygamy. By the early 1890s

---

[263] Maurine Griffith Burmester, Interview.
[264] "C.A. Griffith Fatally Hurt," *Deseret Evening News*, Nov. 8, 1906.

there were 31 Methodist churches in Utah.[265] However, most new members were immigrants and not converts. Consequently, in the financial crisis of 1893 many members left and most of the churches collapsed. Iliff steadfastly remained.

By October1895, Theodore was suffering from heart disease. On Saturday October 5, 1895 Theodore fell ill with a stomach ailment that exacerbated his heart problem. He died late Sunday night. Dr. Iliff fulfilled his agreement with Theodore and delivered the eulogy for his friend.[266]

---

[265] *First United Methodist Church: 130 Years*, 6.
[266] "Theo. Burmester's Funeral," Deseret Evening News, Oct. 8, 1895.

Chapter 10: The Search

On June 3, 2001 my father, Byron Bovee Burmester Jr.,
died from complications of ALS. His whole body had atrophied to
the point where he needed oxygen and a full-time care giver. His
last month or so was a horror. The oxygen mask caused a sore on
the bridge of his nose. As time went on, he became more and more
disoriented, especially at night. At the end, his tired shrunken body
was not strong enough to exhale the carbon dioxide from his
lungs. He slipped into unconsciousness as he struggled to get air,
involuntarily taking rapid shallow gasps. Finally, he quietly died
of asphyxiation, quite a contrast to Theodore's sudden demise.

At the time of my father's death I had previously planned
to go to Slovakia with some friends from my church to teach
English as a second language at a children's English camp
organized by Missions To The World. I was excited about the
opportunity to help these kids who would be the first generation in
their families to enter adulthood in a democratic capitalist
republic. But I was also excited by the prospect of traveling to
Prague afterward because I had been working on a writing project
for several years involving historical Prague.

I still went on the trip—it was about five or six weeks
after the funeral. It was a fantastic experience; the children were so
enthusiastic and their country so beautiful and mysterious. The
countryside and the town from which the kids came was both

ancient and soviet industrial while trying to evolve into something new and modern. Prague too was exciting; to see the places I had been reading and studying about for several years was thrilling. One day we even had a personal guide, an engineer whose hobby was architectural history.

However, when I got back to the States, I could not resume writing my book about Prague. This story about Theodore and Ariminta, which by this time I still only knew scant details, kept barging into my thoughts. Some voice inside me kept animating me, compelling me to research it, to find out more about it.

The following spring, 2002, I arranged a family trip to Washington into which I incorporated a couple hours of research time at the old Idaho Historical Society research library. I was rewarded on that trip when I found the newspaper articles confirming what my Aunt had told me regarding the sexual assault on Ariminta and her murder. But on that same morning at the library I made another discovery, a literally jaw-dropping surprise.

I told the librarian what I was doing and that I had limited time in which to pursue it. So, I asked for advice on how best to use my time. The librarian explained that there had been an elderly volunteer who had worked for years cataloging all the materials in the library. She availed herself of no preexisting system but rather recorded what she thought were important subject matter entries on a card and then placed the card into alphabetical sequence in the catalogue. The librarian said, "Some researchers have found it helpful.' I looked up "Burmester" and found 18 entries. Some dealt with Ariminta's murder, but most were announcements in the newspaper of land transactions and lawsuits commenced by Theodore. However, when I reached the second to the last entry it referenced a newspaper article concerning Theodore's "fatal affray" with Judge Morford. That morning my vector, the path I was on, crossed that of the elderly volunteer who had long before entered the information onto that index card and I, a person unknown to her, benefitted immensely from it.

Following that unexpected discovery, during the long hours of driving to Washington and back I remembered the genealogy work that my Dad's cousin had left at my parents' house. Once I got back in town I went to my mother's home and together we searched until we found those two long brown legal sized folders with the information carefully pronged in them.

Inside one of the two files I found photocopies copies of letters from Wilma Bishop, Hank Burmester, and L.S. Thompson. I also found copies of newspaper clippings profiling Henry (Theodore's younger brother) and Marianne D'Arcy. There was even a copy of Theodore's hand-written letter to Marianne filled with pain detailing Minnie's murder. Although I had lived for years under the same roof with these two folders, reading them for the first time and understanding the significance of their contents was an amazing discovery for me.

Once again, I felt the pull of the investigation. Each of these sources provided remarkable stories regarding the early lives of Theodore and Ariminta. Several referred to William's involvement in a shootout and other stories wild and previously unknown to me. I sent off emails to the Utah Historical Society as well as the Idaho Historical Society to confirm what I could. Through these inquiries I learned of the shooting in Bingham which resolved a conflict in Wilma's and Thompson's accounts of William's shootout with the desperado. On the other hand, I was never able to find any support for Thompson's claim that his grandfather, William Burmester became sheriff in Stevensville, Montana after the Bingham shooting. Moreover, I could find no support for his claim that William had made a principled stand and refused to take up arms against Chief Joseph and the Nez Perce in their flight to Canada.

But what really caught my attention was the claim that Theodore and his brother and perhaps the entire family (excluding the father) walked across the Isthmus of Panama. It caught my attention so immediately and completely because years earlier, long before I had ever heard of Theodore and Ariminta I too had walked across the Isthmus of Panama from Atlantic to Pacific.

<u>I Too Walked the Isthmus</u>

While I was still in college, in 1980, an undergraduate in History and a ROTC cadet, I volunteered to go on active duty in the United States Army as an infantry officer upon graduation. When it came time to submit our assignment preferences to the Department of the Army most of my classmates requested the most popular assignments in Germany or stateside in the golden

triangle: Fort Carson, Colorado, Fort Ord, California, and Fort
Lewis, Washington. Before that time, I had never really
considered the Republic of Panama as a place to live. At the time I
knew very little of my ancestors and did not know a person named
Theodore had existed, much less that he had been to the Isthmus
of Panama before me. But, being young, single and looking for
excitement I requested Panama.

I was assigned to a light infantry battalion on the Pacific
side on a post called Fort Kobbe, which was merely an Army
annex of Howard Air Force Base. When I arrived, the United
States was rapidly approaching the end of its direct involvement in
the Republic of Panama, but at the time still maintained a number
of small installations on both sides of the Isthmus and on each side
of the Canal. Fort Davis and Fort Sherman were on the Atlantic
while Forts Clayton, Kobbe, and Amador as well as Howard Air
Force Base were on the Pacific. Fort Kobbe was on the opposite
side of the canal from Panama City, Fort Clayton (the main
headquarters of our parent unit the 193d Brigade) and Fort
Amador (headquarters of Southern Command).

It was a fantastic assignment for a young infantry officer
as it turned out, just what I had sought, full of tough realistic
training in a jungle environment. When my Army chartered
airliner landed at Howard Air Force Base with all the other
"cherries" I was first struck by the heat, the air so thick it felt like
you could touch it. There was no breeze, and that thick hot air
clung to my dark green class "A" uniform. It was January, the

depth of the winter where I had come from and yet the hillsides surrounding the airstrip were lush and green. December in Panama was the end of the rainy season and any open spaces like nearby Venado Drop Zone were thickly overgrown with dense ten-foot-tall stands of "cuna grass." Over the next two years I learned that by March, during the height of dry season, when Theodore would have crossed the Isthmus, the cuna grass burns off leaving open fields of stubble. The grass fires fill valleys with a grey haze and the acrid smell of burning grass.

In February of my first year, the Brigade launched its semiannual field exercise and my company was designated OPFOR, opposition forces, irregular style guerrillas, and I got my first close look at the most dramatic difference between the Panama that I saw, and that which Theodore had seen in 1853: the Panama Canal. Much of the canal is a reservoir created by a dam on the Chagres River. For the exercise my company was positioned on what would have been a hilltop in Theodore's day, but was a peninsula that extended into the lake when I went there. On my first night in the jungle the sun went down around 6:30 as it did every evening all year long. Once the sun went down it was black, I mean the complete absence of light, such that when I held my hand inches from my face, I could not make out my hand. During the course of the next two weeks I learned about local flora that I should avoid like ant trees, small fern-like bushes usually four or five feet high so called because they were the exclusive residence of a small but vicious variety of ant, and black palm, a tree that I remember little about except that it had a two to three inch diameter trunk that was thickly protected by sharp gray fragile spines that went deep into one's hand when one was foolish enough to grasp the trunk. The spines would instantly break off and cause a painful local infection. Near the end of that exercise my company was ordered to leave our well-hidden encampment on the peninsula and walk through the jungle to another location. We packed our equipment into our ruck sacks in absolute darkness and awaited the order to move. I sat at my command post position resting against my ruck sack when something suddenly ran across my lap. To this day I have no idea what it was. I suspect a monkey, but it was silent and ran on four legs that felt like the size and weight of a house cat.

On another training exercise I recall my platoon operating in the jungle on Fort Sherman on the Atlantic side. Fort Sherman was a large training area for Panama, that included a wide area from White Drop Zone, an old sugar cane field near the reservoir between the dam and the locks on the south, to the mouth of the Chagres on the north including Fort San Lorenzo and from Limon Bay on the east where the several buildings of the garrison were located to some considerable distance into the jungle on the opposite side of the river on the west. On this occasion my platoon was stationed on a high plateau. Small streams plunged down through the jungle over great white boulders to the Chagres River below. I count it among the most beautiful places I have ever had the good fortune to see. One day in the distance I could hear a screaming kind of barking noise which I had never heard before. The screams continued unabated for some time before I finally asked one of my soldiers what that infernal noise was, to which they replied, "Sir, that is a howler monkey." I have since seen howler monkeys in our local zoo. They are a small slender brown monkey, cute but really unremarkable in appearance from other species of monkey. However, that noise they make—howling—is amazing. That such a slight little monkey could produce such an enormous sound is truly remarkable.

In September or October of my second year in Panama my battalion went to Fort Sherman yet again, this time to attend the Army's Jungle Warfare School and then to participate in a large-scale tactical training exercise. After the exercise was over my battalion walked the fifty or so miles back across the Isthmus to Fort Kobbe. I remember my battalion commander who had been injured in a serious helicopter crash during the exercise nevertheless led us back walking with the help of a cane and carrying a jar of Atlantic Ocean water which he ceremoniously added to the Pacific upon our arrival. Like some of the travelers in the early 1850s we took the rail lines for much of the first half of the trip, only we just used the tracks as a path on which to walk. It was a horrible march along the tracks; the ties were at an uncomfortable distance, too far for an easy stride but too close for a wide quick pace.

Our trek across the Isthmus was miserable. Of course, it was hot, but we walked mostly at night to avoid heat injuries and had our logistical trains that could re-supply us with water or anything else we needed, while evacuating casualties who could no longer continue the march due to heat or foot injuries. I am certain that Theodore had no such luxuries. The most important difference between my experience and that of Theodore's had nothing to do with the canal, train tracks or logistical support, however. What made my trek so different from Theodore's, one could not see with the naked eye. But it was a difference that meant life or death to those thousands of rail workers who died building the railroad across the Isthmus in the 1850's. By the time I arrived in 1982 malaria had been all but eradicated and we, soldiers, had been immunized from plague and yellow fever.

Another Discovery

On Monday, May 31, 2004, Memorial Day, I experienced another emotional breakthrough. I was working in my yard and I was thinking about what had become of Theodore's body, after all he had died here in Salt Lake City. It seemed to me as I thought about it, there were two old cemeteries in town, Salt Lake City Cemetery and Mt. Olivet Cemetery. It also was my belief that the Salt Lake City Cemetery was traditionally a Latter-day Saint cemetery while Mt. Olivet was the resting place for deceased "gentiles." So, at about 2:30 on that afternoon I called Mt. Olivet and asked if they had a record of Theodore Burmester. They replied almost immediately that he was buried there. However, I needed to go there soon because the office, with its master map, closed at 4:00 p.m. Consequently, I leaped into my car and drove directly to the cemetery. It was only a short, fifteen-minute, drive from my house to Mt. Olivet.

When I arrived, I stopped briefly at the office to receive directions to the location and look at the map. I found the location and parked my car. As I approached, I could see a large granite upright marker with the name "Burmester" carved into it. Next to it was a large floral wreath someone had anonymously sent. Beneath them lay the gravestones of Theodore, Maria Finch and three of their daughters. I felt a sudden surge, a rush of gratification. I had finally found something that was not just a story recorded but something tangible that I could actually reach out and touch.

In my spare time I took to looking for clues on the internet. The following year I found The Maritime Heritage Project, a reference web site "established by D. Blethen Adams Levy in 1998 to preserve maritime history during the 1800s with a focus on the port of San Francisco." The site has various documents entered into a searchable database. It was in this interesting collection that I found the name "T. Burmester" amongst the passengers who had submitted the complimentary card following the grounding of the SS Tennessee. The name "A. Barmester" on the passenger manifest resolved for me the conflict between Hank Burmester's letter and the newspaper profile of Theodore's younger brother, Henry.

It was also on the internet that I discovered Marianne D'Arcy had written a memoir and that the manuscript was held in the University of Oregon Library in Eugene. The hunt had me transfixed once again. It was as though I now knew where a hidden treasure was "buried" and I had to go and dig it up. So, in 2006, on fairly short notice I was able to schedule a week-long holiday for my family to Newport, Oregon during my daughter's spring break. We all drove up to Oregon and as it turned out our beloved "Red Rocks," the University of Utah Gymnastics Team, was participating in the NCAA championship at the same time at Corvallis, Oregon. The vacation was perfect.

On the way to Oregon we made another stop in Boise for several hours of research, in the new, state-of-the-art, historical society building. I checked my bag at the wall locker and went into a special climate-controlled room. There a librarian retrieved a box with original documents from the Morford homicide trial! There were hand-written court documents, affidavits etc. It was like walking into a fold in time to be able to look directly upon these documents that had been filed in 1869. I could, to my surprise, look through them although I could only touch them with clean white gloves.

We soon were on the road again. I drove up to Mount Vernon, Washington to visit family for the weekend before shoving off to Newport. On Friday of that following week I rented a car so I could drive down to Eugene while my family enjoyed the beach. The campus was beautiful. Everything in Oregon is green and thickly vegetated, at least on the western side. I found Marianne's "Remembrances" in the special collections in Knight

Library. Seeing the original manuscript which had been typed on an old typewriter gave me that same sensation of stepping back in time. Although the manuscript had not been created directly from the hands of Ariminta, it was pretty close. It was so exciting to see those pages, typed probably by D'Arcy's daughter, lifting her voice from the past and putting it down on the page now before me. Most importantly the contents were indeed a treasure. I am sure I grinned from ear to ear as I drove back to Newport with my prize photocopies.

Just as was the case with Marianne's memoir I was able to glean much information about Theodore and Ariminta from others who were close to them. Wilma Bishop in her letter described the extremely close bonds of friendship Theodore and Thomas Corwin Iliff, the Methodist missionary, shared. I was able to confirm her assertion, at least to some degree, when I found the obituary reporting that Dr. Iliff had performed Theodore's funeral service. I went to the present day First United Methodist Church and asked them about Dr. Iliff. They gave me a booklet chronicling their church's history. From it I gleaned that though I had never heard of him, in Theodore's day he was a man of some national renown and so again I went back on-line. I learned that in Colorado there is a Methodist Seminary called the Iliff School of Theology. Although the school is not named after him, it is named for the principal donor, John Wesley Iliff, Thomas' wealthy rancher cousin, the school nevertheless has a strong connection to the Missionary to the Rocky Mountains. Initially, the school library guided me to the Gillilan book, *Thomas Corwin Iliff, Apostle of the Home Missions in the Rocky Mountains*. However, as I was finishing up the first draft of this manuscript, I thought I should check again. Since my first contact, Laura, an archivist at the school, informed me that they had recently received correspondence and other papers of Thomas Corwin Iliff from one of his heirs. She looked through the new file but unfortunately did not find any correspondence to or from Theodore Burmester. However, after first obtaining permission she put me in contact with Iliff's heir, a great-grandson named Michael. I eagerly called Michael, left a message and to my surprise and delight he returned my call the same day. We had a splendid conversation and he promised to peruse his remaining papers from Thomas Corwin. He also shared with me a priceless "vector" story not unlike my own. He had been stationed with the military in "fair" Verona, Italy and during that time had occasions to take the train on business that ultimately winds its way to Rome. Years later when reading parts of Thomas Corwin's diary, he learned that Thomas Corwin had also taken that same rail line to Rome during his European sabbatical. I shared my "vector" story from my days in Panama with Michael and we marveled that we each shared such similar déjà vu-like connections to our ancestors through our own military service.

Five or six years after I began this project I had very little direct evidence of Theodore's actions and beliefs once he arrived in Utah other than the shoot-out in Bingham. I knew he had been a lawyer, so I searched on a legal search engine for "Burmester" and discovered that he had been named counsel on appeal in at least seventeen cases. Of those, three were criminal cases and the rest civil cases. As I looked into the criminal cases I found a thesis paper published online dealing with one of those cases, People v. Brigham Young Hampton. The thesis paper cited to Jeffrey Nichols's "Prostitution, Polygamy, and Power." From both the thesis paper and Nichols's book it was obvious their original source was the newspaper accounts. So, I went to our local library and found that the coverage was amazingly detailed. Although voir dire and jury selection are important to our system of justice it is so dull to the casual observer you would choose to have your tooth drilled without Novocain rather than read about or watch jury selection. Nevertheless, there was so much local interest in the case that the newspapers' reportage even covered the jury selection in detail.

It has been nearly twenty years since I first began looking to corroborate those family stories. A lot has changed since then. Not much of it totally unexpected. My father and my grandmother died soon after I began the project. Later, my beautiful loving mother died. She had a stroke one day and fell. She quietly died several days later. It is in bitter submission to the relentless consequences of the passage of time that I find myself unable to share this story with those who I most wish to share it.

Although those sources have been silenced for all time, what I found in the ensuing years has amazed me. Some of that amazement I see in the substance, but I am also amazed at how easy it was to find, as if it was placed in front of me so that I could not help but stumble upon it, wake up from my stupor, and recognize it for what it was. For example, the initial research by my father's cousin, a Latter-day Saint doing his duty, is not in itself startling. But he passed the fruit of that research on to my father who had long before renounced his mother's faith and had no interest in genealogy and baptizing the dead. Nevertheless, he kept the documents, tucked into a corner on the shelf, untouched for years, until I came back from my trip to Washington.

If the ease of the search surprised me, it was the joy of finding such unusual and colorful characters under each "stone" that I picked up and turned over that provided the excitement for the search itself. Each new discovery left me like a treasure hunter always wanting to get back to look for more. But the question that plagues me is, why did the enticement of the search excite me so? Was it just the satisfaction of completing a puzzle, like finding the hidden differences between two apparently identical photographs but one of which has been slightly altered?

Other than the years that I spent in the army I have lived nearly all my life, a "gentile," in Salt Lake City, the land of "Zion." Every July 24 amidst the celebration of "Days of '47" I have felt the nagging frustration of that celebration. Partly the frustration derives from the scope of the celebration that dwarfs that of Independence Day as it is celebrated in Utah. A central part of the "Days of '47" celebration is a parade in the city. In the parade there are the usual political leaders, police motorcycle squads and clowns, but the focus of the parade is the celebration of the Latter-day Saint immigrants with a token nod to the indigenous people. My mother loathed this celebration and so instead of taking us kids to the parade, she took my sister and I to the swimming club.

Since my return to Utah I have found this state-sanctioned holiday reveling in the glorification of the Latter-day Saint pioneers really wearing on me, because though I didn't know how my family got here, I was quite certain it was not with a Latter-day Saint wagon train. Now I know. I am here because Theodore's beloved Ariminta, my great-great-grandmother, was murdered and when Theodore's life suddenly turned into a train wreck he wanted to start over. Today, through this search I have found out how it was that my people came to the Great Basin. I can still get frustrated with the single-minded scope of the 24th celebration but I now have my own story. The search for my own story was what really drew me in. It was not just a desire to solve a mystery for the sake of solving it—it was to find my place here in Zion.

My family story like everyone's story has many facets. Some are bright and clear like that of Ariminta mortally wounded, a modern-day Lucretia, who's first thought was not of herself but of her baby that she believed was still in the burning house. Other facets are dark like Theodore's pointless duel with Judge Morford. Other parts of the story shine simply because the participants struggled and fought through incredible hardships. But through it all, it is my story, my family story, the history of my fathers…and mothers. It is a sacred trust that I will pass on to my daughter; of how we, Burmesters, came to be here at this time. On July 24 we won't be walking in the parade, and we certainly won't have our own float, but I will be satisfied, because by searching and uncovering my family story I have learned not only about them but who I am. I am Fred Burmester son of Byron and Barbara, son of Byron and Maurine, son of Frank and Emma, the son of Theodore and Ariminta.

BIBLIOGRAPHY

Books:

Arrington, Leonard J. *History of Idaho*, vol. 1. Moscow: University of Idaho Press. 1994.

Bagley, Will. *Blood of Prophets: Brigham Young and the Massacre at Mountain Meadows*. Norman: University of Oklahoma Press. 2002.

Bailey, Lynn R. *Old Reliable: A History of Bingham Canyon, Utah*. Tucson: Western Lore Press. 1988.

Baltzell, E. Digby. *Puritan Boston and Quaker Philadelphia: Two Protestant Ethics and the Spirit of Class Authority and Leadership*. New York: The Free Press, 1979.

Baskin, Robert Newton. *Reminiscences of Early Utah*. Salt Lake City: Baskin. 1914.

Blanthorn, Ouida. *A History of Tooele County*. Salt Lake City: Utah State Historical Society. 1998.

Bowman, Carl and Kraybill, Donald B. *On the Backroad to Heaven: Old Order Hutterites, Mennonites, Amish, and Brethren*, Baltimore: The John Hopkins University Press. 2001.

Brodie, Fawn M. *No Man Knows My History: The Life of Joseph Smith the Mormon Prophet*, 2nd ed. New York: Vintage Books. 1995.

Bushman, Richard Lyman. *Joseph Smith: Rough Stone Rolling*. New York: Alfred A. Knopf. 2005.

Donaldson, Thomas. *Idaho of Yesterday*. Westport: Greenwood Press. 1970.

Durham, Nelson Wayne. *History of Spokane and Spokane County.* Spokane: The S. J. Clarke Publishing Co. 1912.

Foote, Shelby. *The Civil War A Narrative: Red River to Appomattox.* New York: Random House Inc. 1974.

Geffen, Elizabeth M. "Industrial Development and Social Crisis 1841-1854," in *Philadelphia: A 300-Year History.* Edited by Russell F. Weigley et. al. New York: W. W. Norton and Co. 307-61. 1982.

Gillilan, James David. *Thomas Corwin Iliff: Apostle of Home Missions in the Rocky Mountains.* New York: The Methodist Book Concern. 1919.

Grant, Ulysses S. *Memoires and Selected Letters.* New York: Literary Classics of the United States, Inc. 1990.

Hamilton, W. D. *In at the Death, or the Last Shot at the Confederacy, Sketches of War History, 1861-1865...* vol. 6, Edited by Brevet Colonel Theodore F. Allen et. al. Wilmington: Broadfoot Publishing Company. 1908.

Hunsaker, Q. Maurice, & Haws, Gwen Hunsaker, eds. *History of Abraham Hunsaker and His Family.* Salt Lake City: Hunsaker Family Organization. 1957.

Kemble, John Haskell. *The Panama Route: 1848-1869.* Columbia: University of South Carolina Press. 1990.

Livy. *The History of Early Rome.* Translated by Aubry de Selincourt. Norwalk: Easton Press. 1988.

McCullough, David. *The Path Between the Seas: The Creation of the Panama Canal 1870-1917.* New York: Simon and Schuster. 1977.

McPherson, James M. *Battle Cry of Freedom: The Civil War Era.* New York: Oxford University Press. 1988.

Nichols, Jeffrey. *Prostitution, Polygamy, and Power: Salt Lake City, 1847-1918.* Urbana: University of Illinois Press. 2002.

Reid, Whitelaw. *Ohio in the War: Her Statesmen, Her Generals, and Soldiers, vol 2.* Cincinnati: Moore, Wilstach, & Baldwin. 1868.

Sherman, William Tecumseh. *Memoirs of General W. T. Sherman.* New York: Literary Classics of the United States, Inc. 1990.

Sutcliffe, Andrea. *Steam: The Untold Story of America's First Great Invention.* New York: Palgrave MacMillan. 2004.

Talmage, James E. *Articles of Faith, Classics in Mormon Literature.* Salt Lake City: Deseret Book Company. 1981.

Wells, Merle W. *Idaho: An Illustrated History.* Boise: The Idaho State Historical Society. 1976.

Whitney, Orson F. *History of Utah in Four Volumes, vol. 4 Biographical*, Salt Lake City: George Q. Cannon and Sons. 1904.

Pamphlets and Periodicals:

Kristensen, Debra K. "The First 50 Men in Idaho Law." *The Advocate.* 53, no. 10 (2010): 54-60.

McBride, John R. "Pioneer Days in the Mountains." *Tullidge's Quarterly Magazine.* 3, no. 3 (1884): 311-320.

First United Methodist Church, 130 Years, Salt Lake City: First United Methodist Church (2000).

"Ganahl the Orator." *Idaho Legal History Society Newsletter.* 1, no. 2 (2009): 3.

James S. Reynolds. Idaho State Historical Society Reference Series. no. 593 (1981).

"Recent Deaths." *The American Lawyer.* 6 (1898): 309.

Court Decisions:

People v. Hampton, 4 Utah 259 (1886).

Manuscripts and Journal Transcripts:

Clark, Joshua Reuben Sr. "Journal Transcriptions." L. Tom Perry Special Collections, Harold B. Lee Library, Brigham Young University (2005).

D'Arcy, Marianne. "Reminiscences." Unpublished Memoir, edited by Daisy Sanford. University of Oregon Special Collections. (1900).

Electronic Sources:

California maritime history, by D. A. Levy.
https://www.maritimeheritage.org/passengers/tn030653.html.

9th Ohio Cavalry, compiled by Larry Stevens.
http://www.ohiocivilwar.com/cwc9.html

Frederic M. Miller, Philadelphia: Immigrant City.
http://www2.hsp.org/exhibits/Balch%20resources/phila_ellis_island.html.

Panama Railroad.
http://web.archive.org/web/20061113105153/http://www.eraofthe clipperships.com/page62.html

INDEX

CPSIA information can be obtained
at www.ICGtesting.com
Printed in the USA
LVHW020353091120
671124LV00017B/631

9 780788 459504